GRAPHIKAL ZEN

AN ADINKRA SYMBOL
ADULT COLORING BOOK

Printed in the United States of America

ISBN 9781081851194

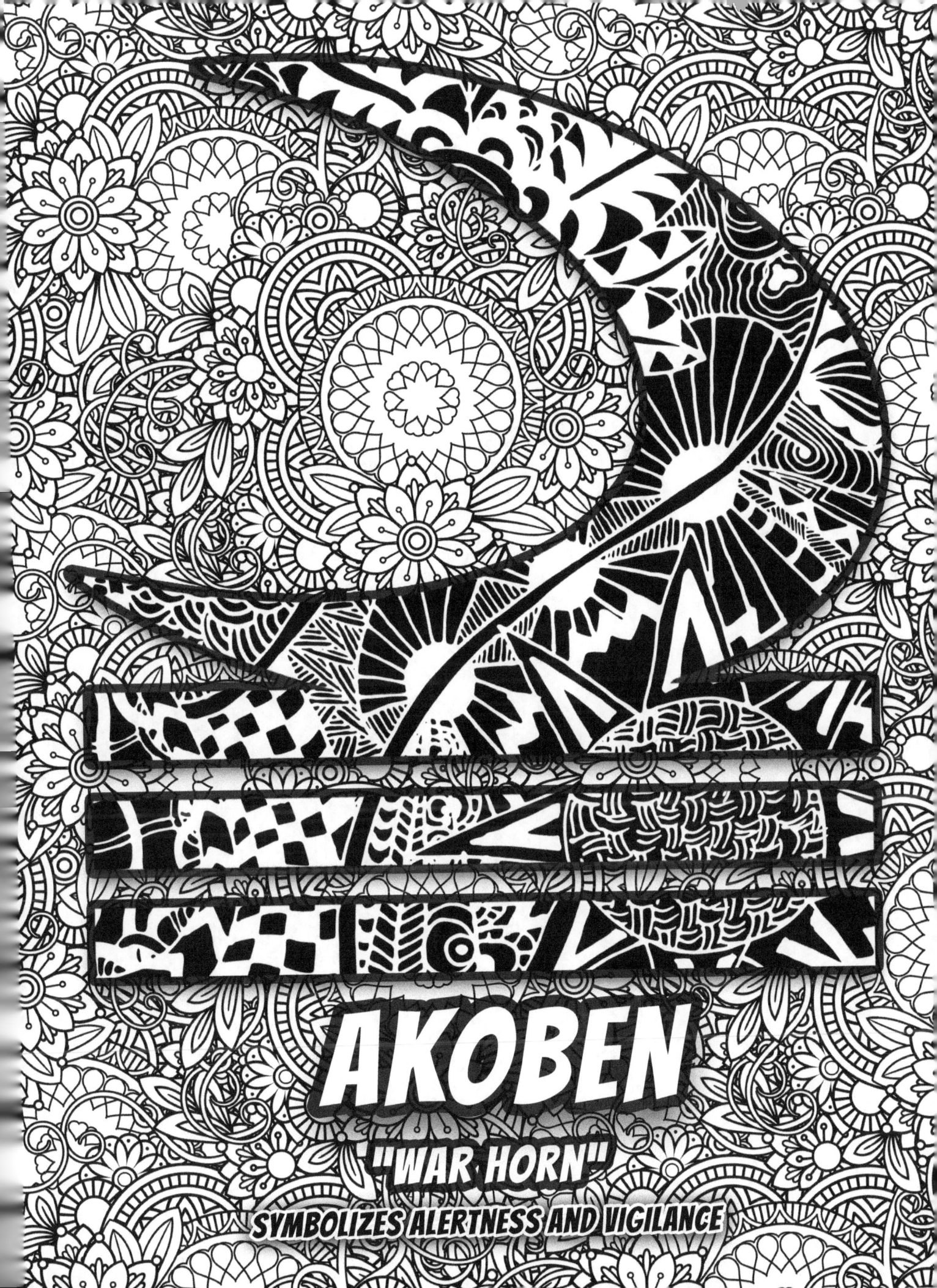

AKOBEN

"WAR HORN"

SYMBOLIZES ALERTNESS AND VIGILANCE

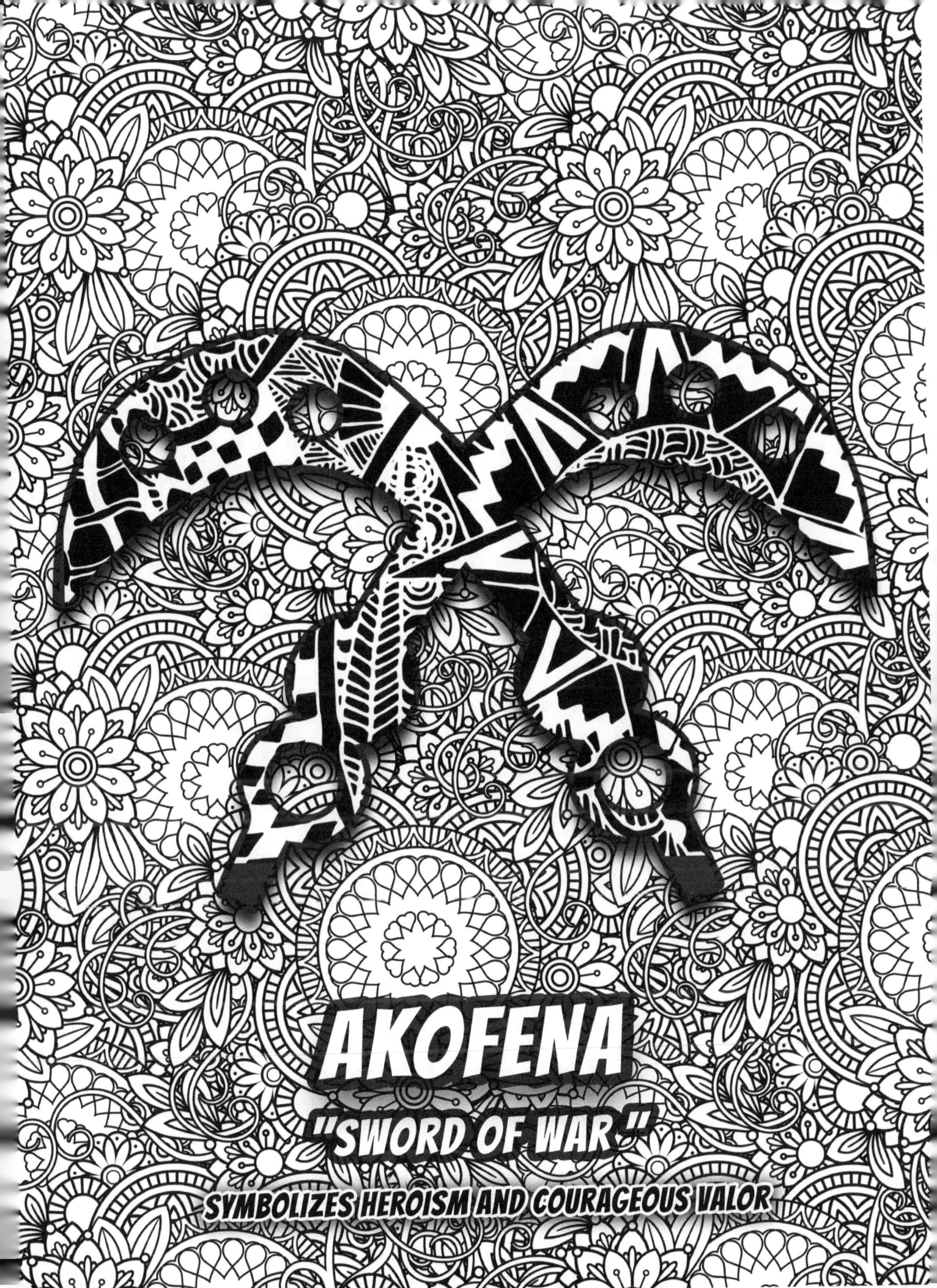

AKOFENA

"SWORD OF WAR"

SYMBOLIZES HEROISM AND COURAGEOUS VALOR

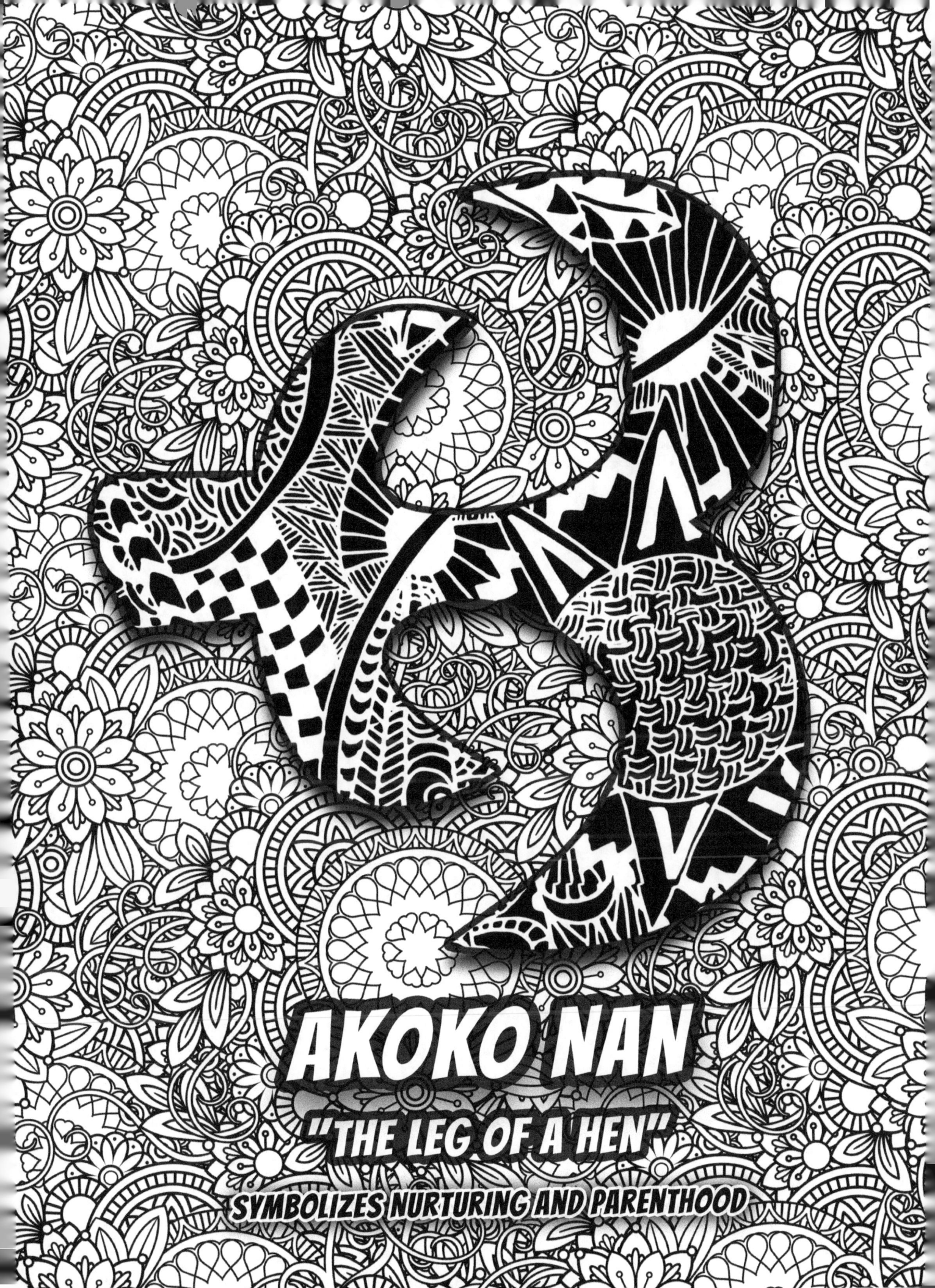

AKOKO NAN

"THE LEG OF A HEN"

SYMBOLIZES NURTURING AND PARENTHOOD

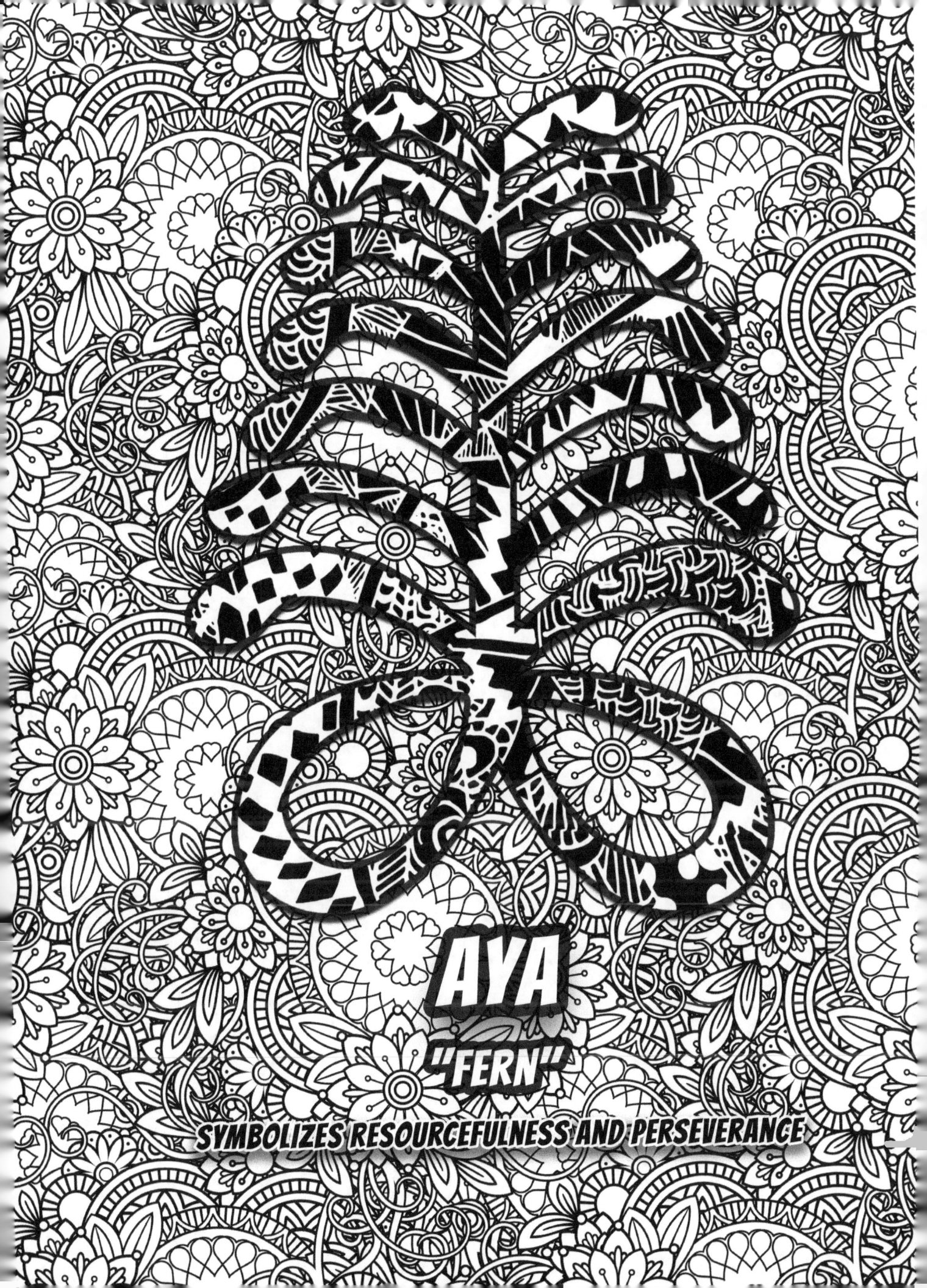

AYA

"FERN"

SYMBOLIZES RESOURCEFULNESS AND PERSEVERANCE

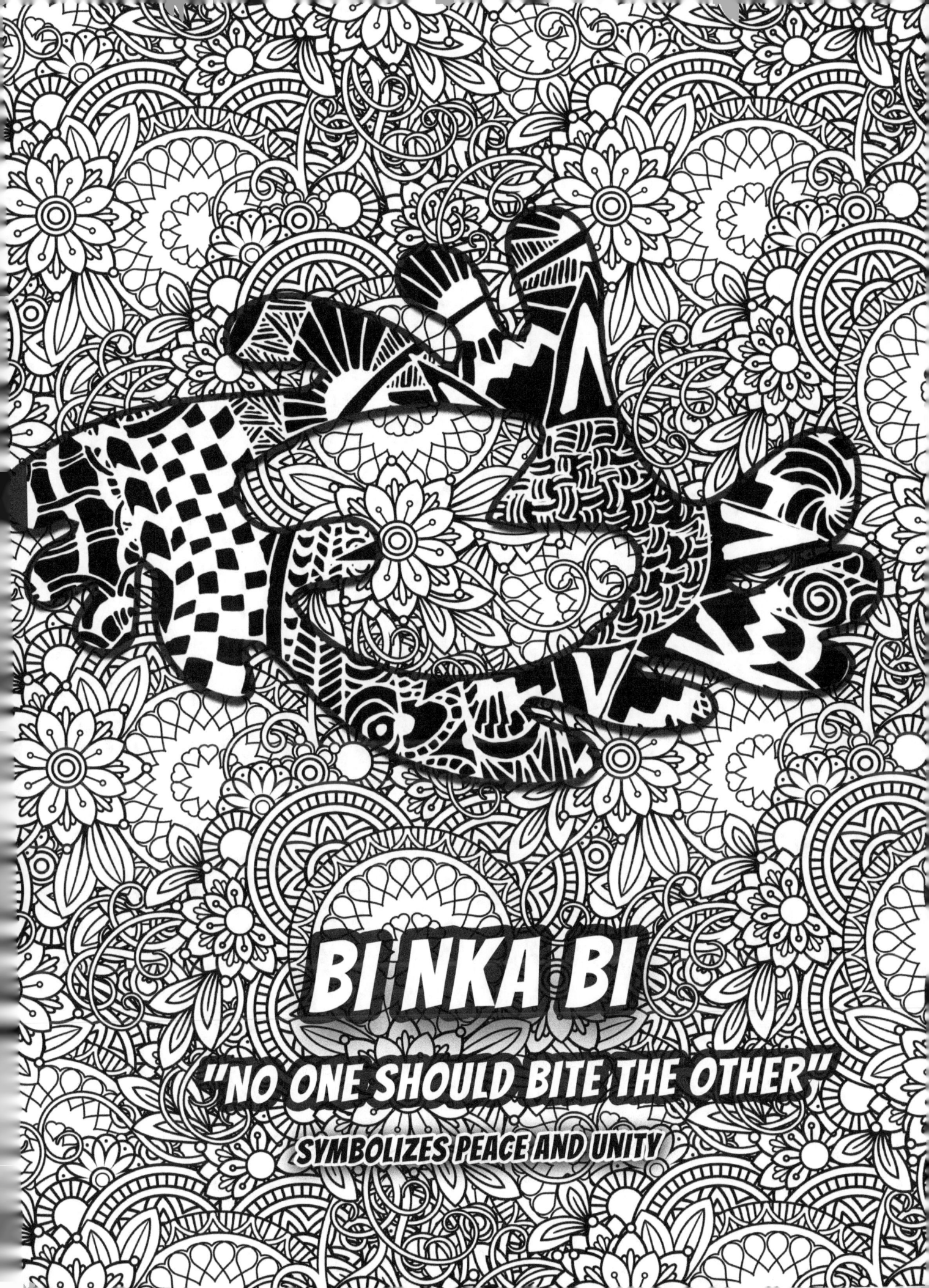

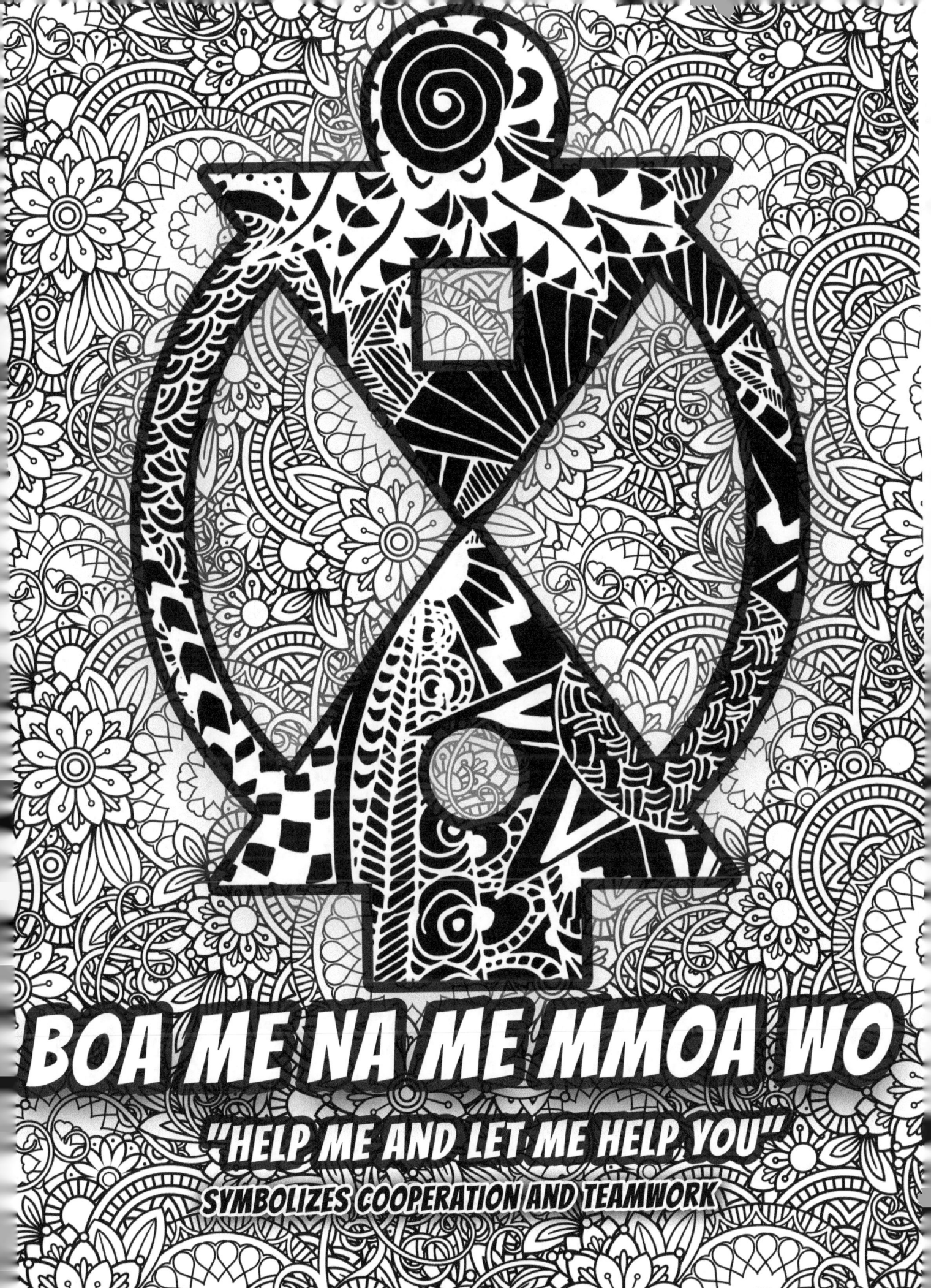

BOA ME NA ME MMOA WO

"HELP ME AND LET ME HELP, YOU"

SYMBOLIZES COOPERATION AND TEAMWORK

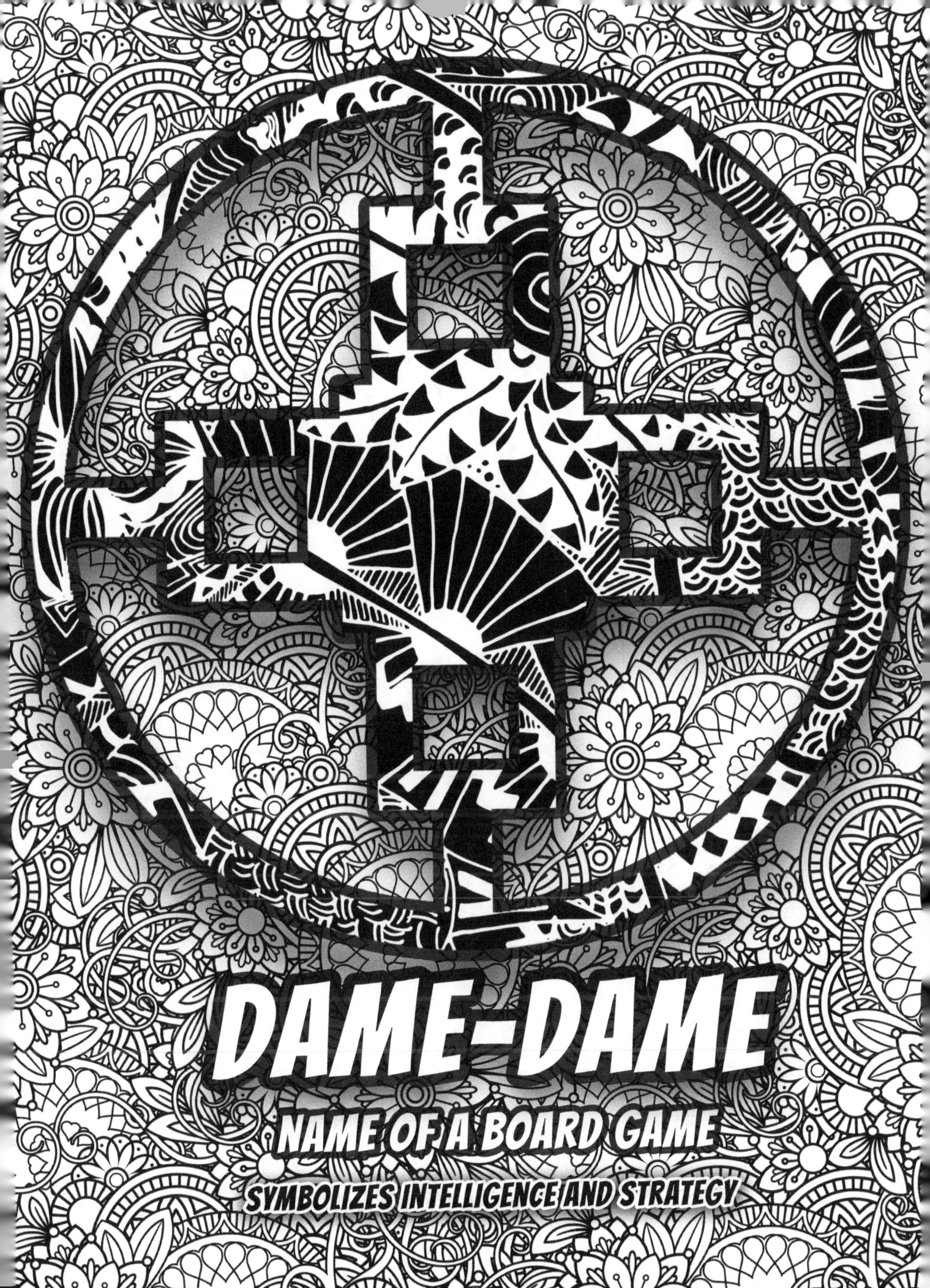

DAME-DAME

NAME OF A BOARD GAME

SYMBOLIZES INTELLIGENCE AND STRATEGY

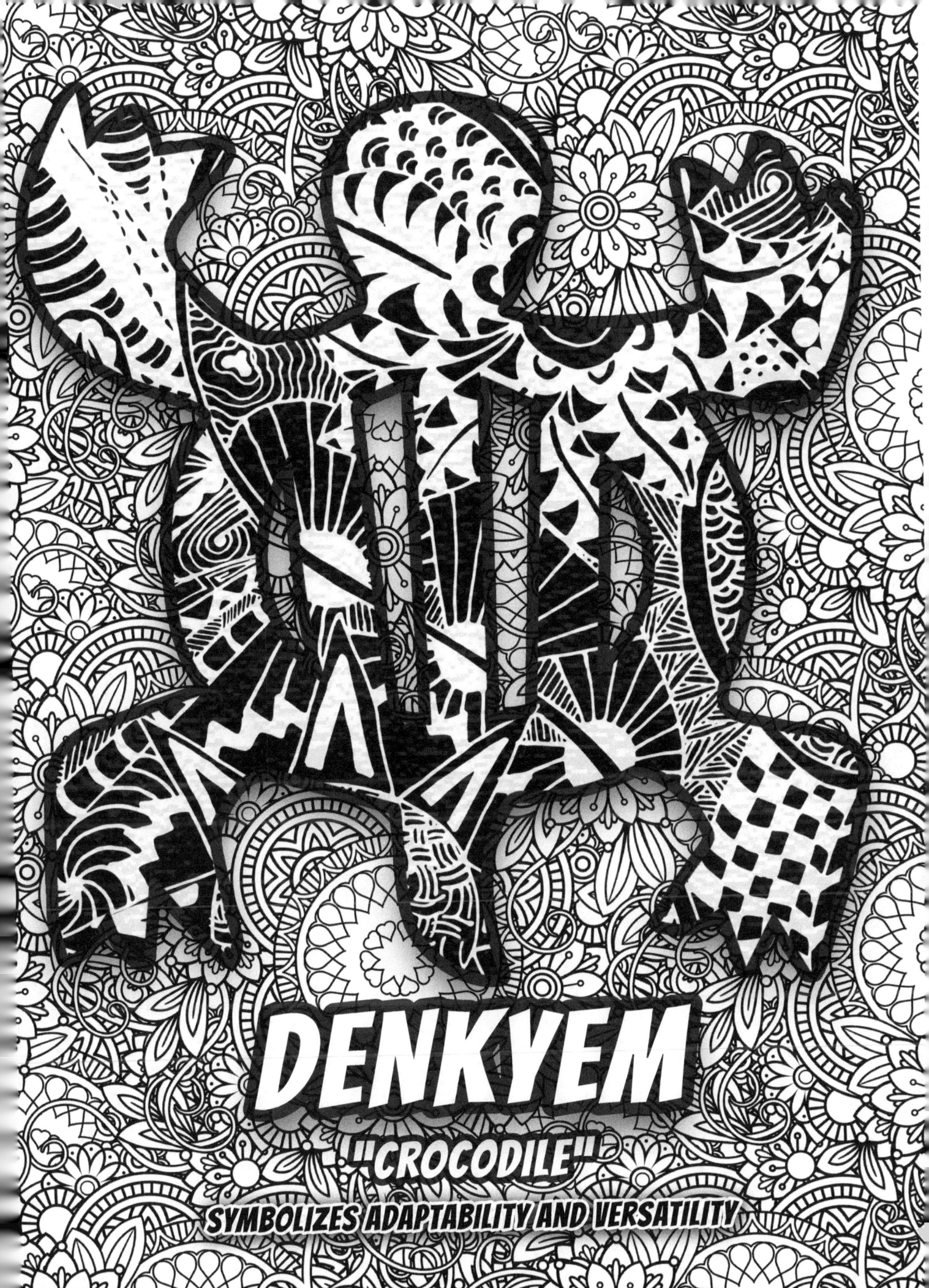

DENKYEM

"CROCODILE"

SYMBOLIZES ADAPTABILITY AND VERSATILITY

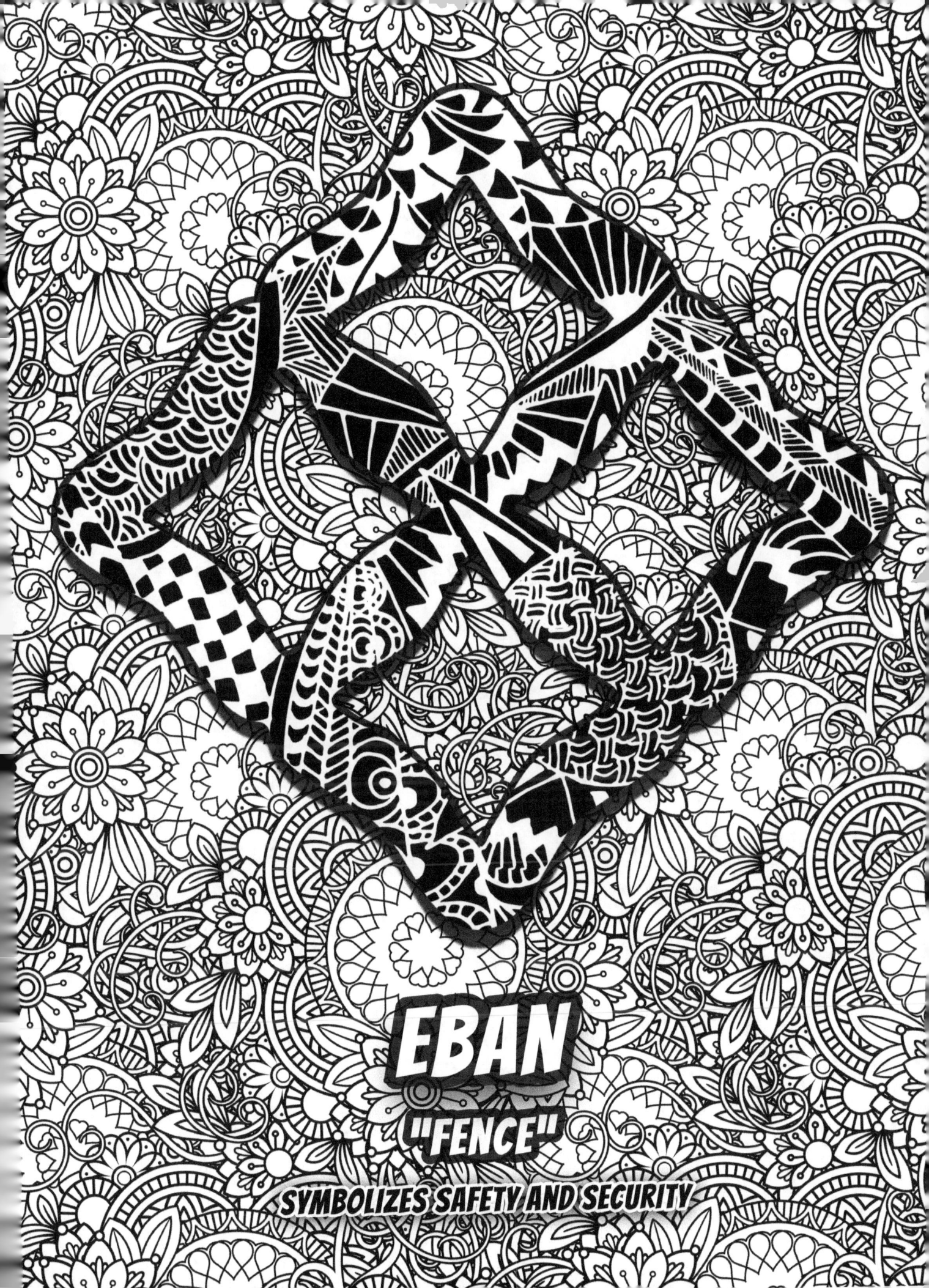

EBAN

"FENCE"

SYMBOLIZES SAFETY AND SECURITY

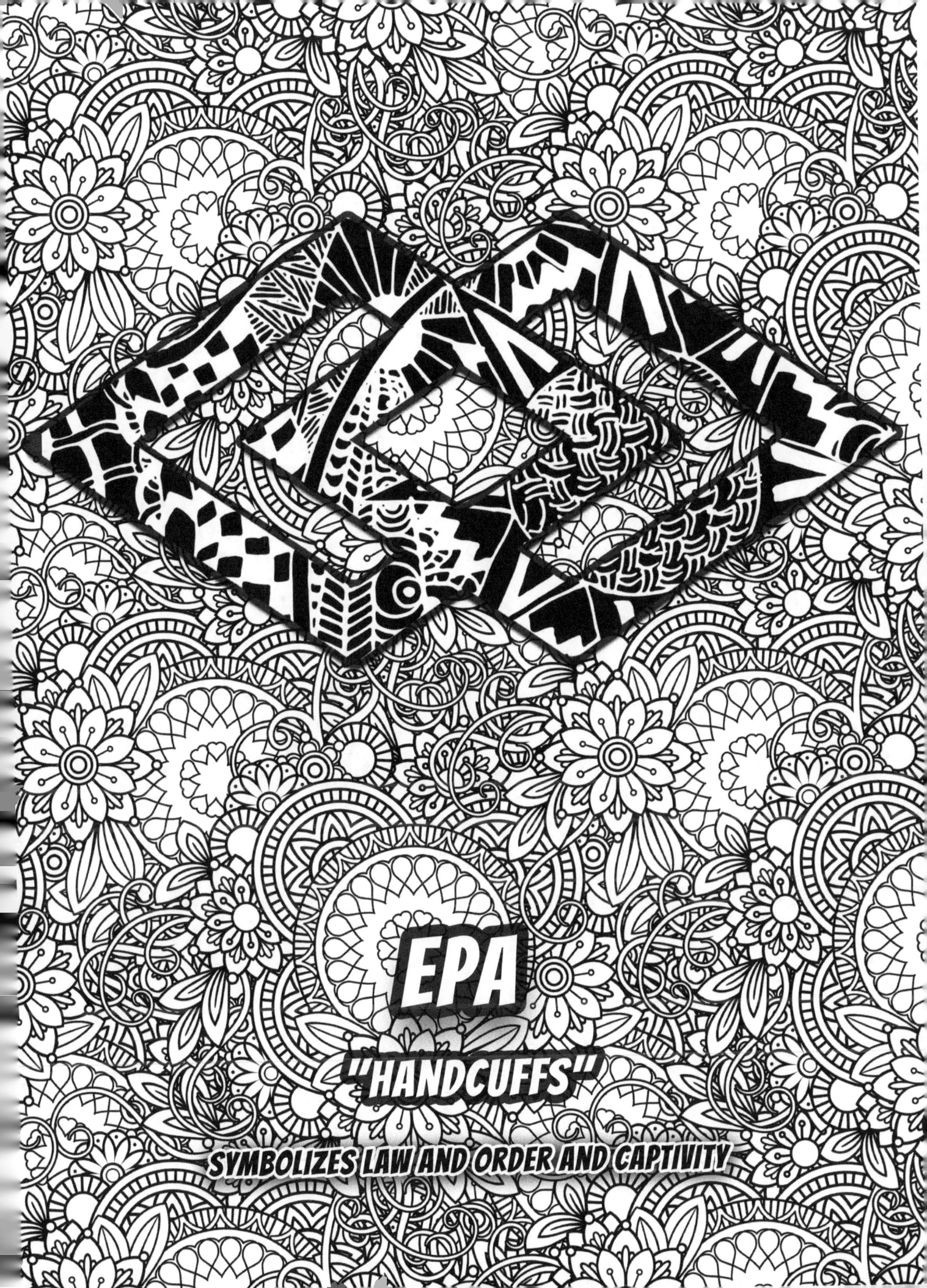

EPA

"HANDCUFFS"

SYMBOLIZES LAW AND ORDER AND CAPTIVITY

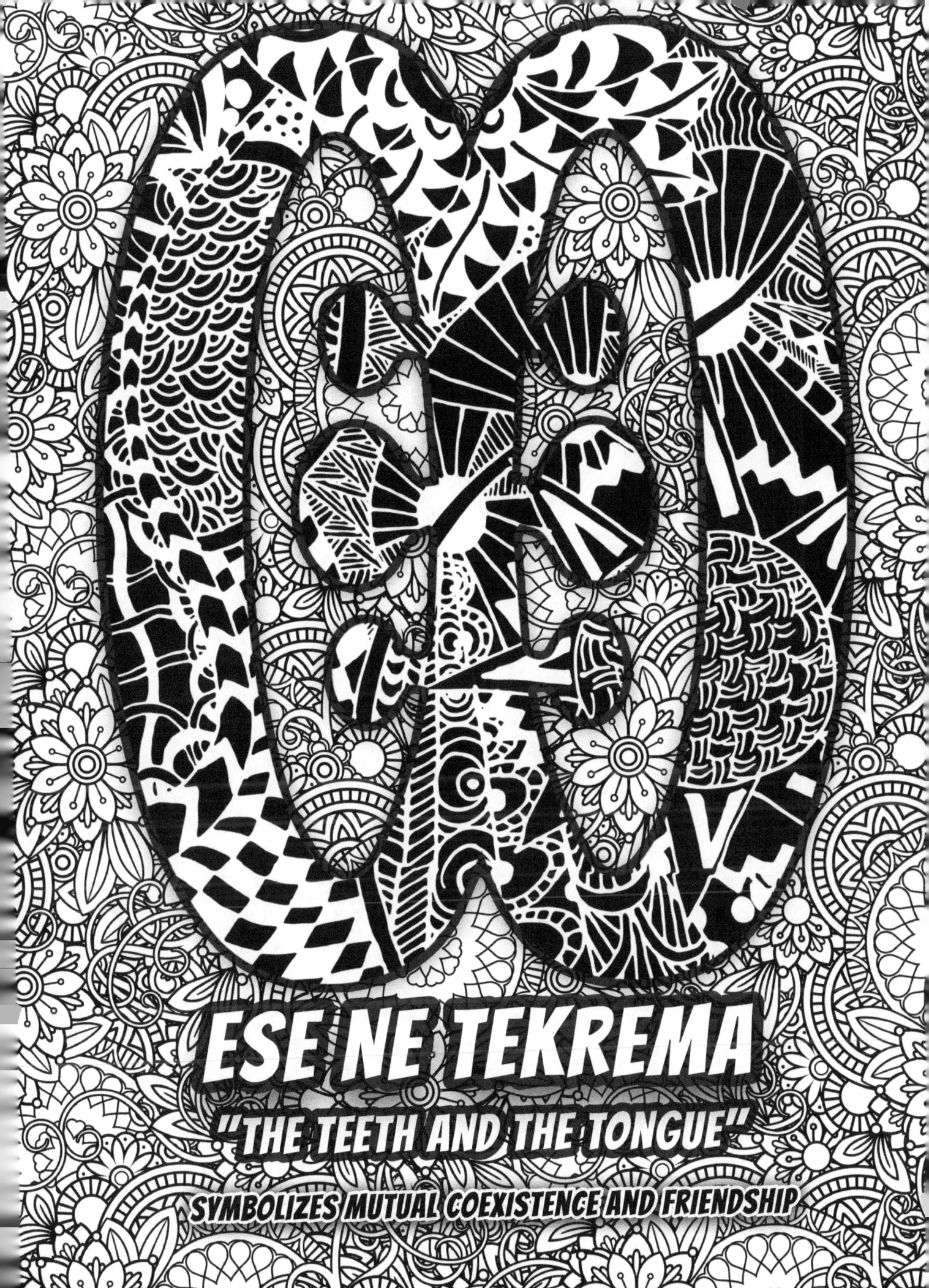

ESE NE TEKREMA
"THE TEETH AND THE TONGUE"
SYMBOLIZES MUTUAL COEXISTENCE AND FRIENDSHIP

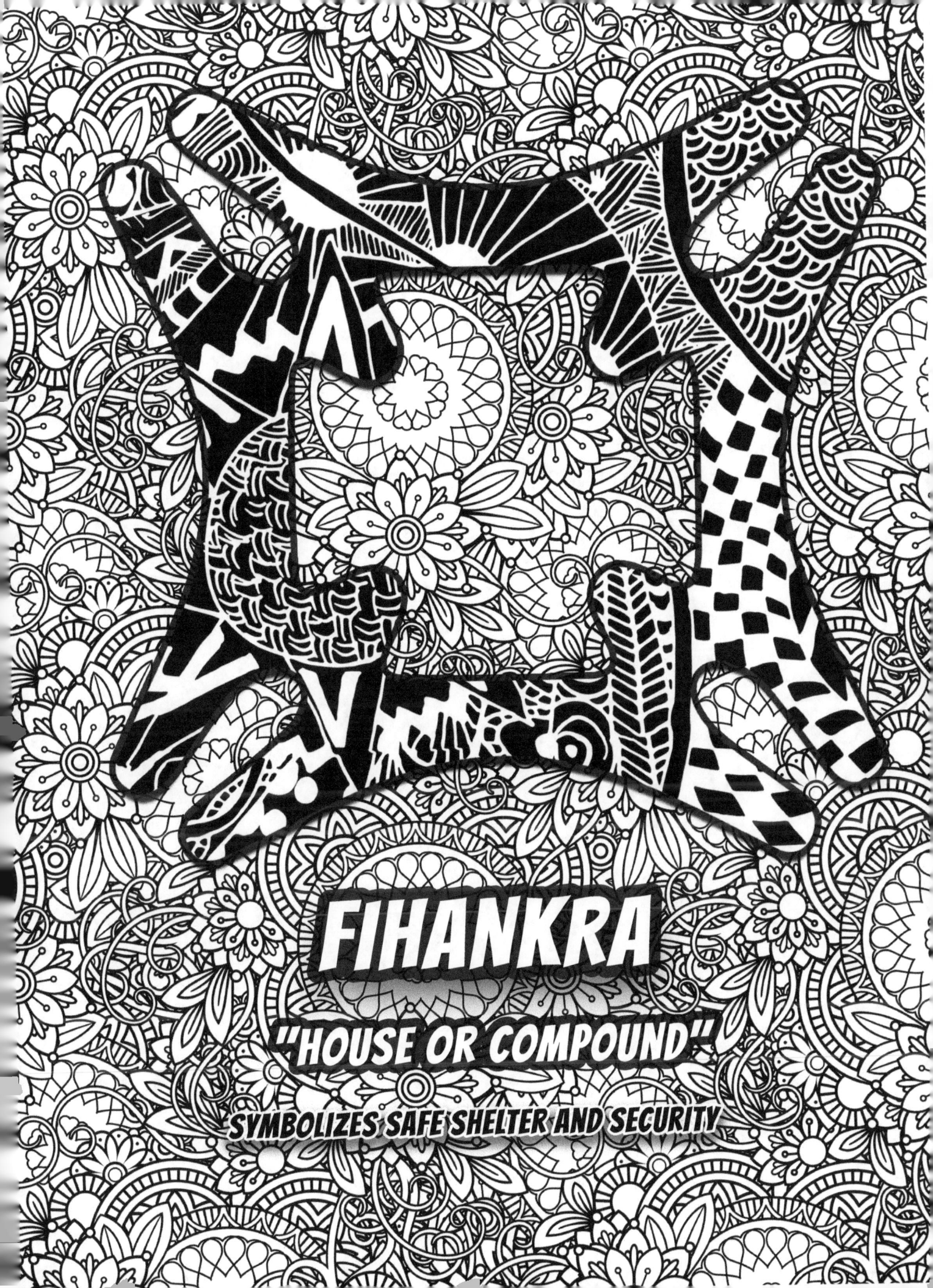

FIHANKRA

"HOUSE OR COMPOUND"

SYMBOLIZES SAFE SHELTER AND SECURITY

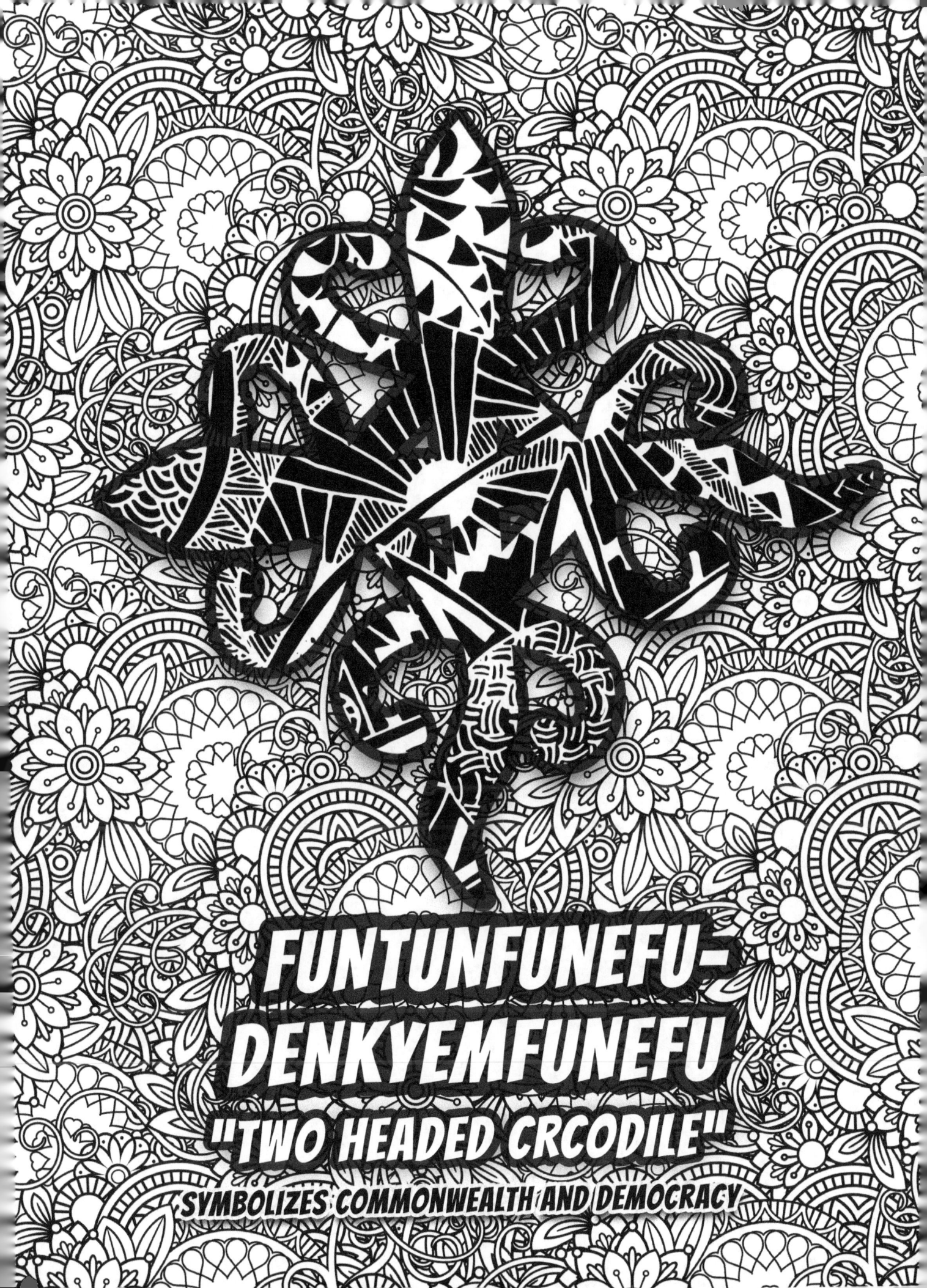

FUNTUNFUNEFU-DENKYEMFUNEFU

"TWO HEADED CRCODILE"

SYMBOLIZES COMMONWEALTH AND DEMOCRACY

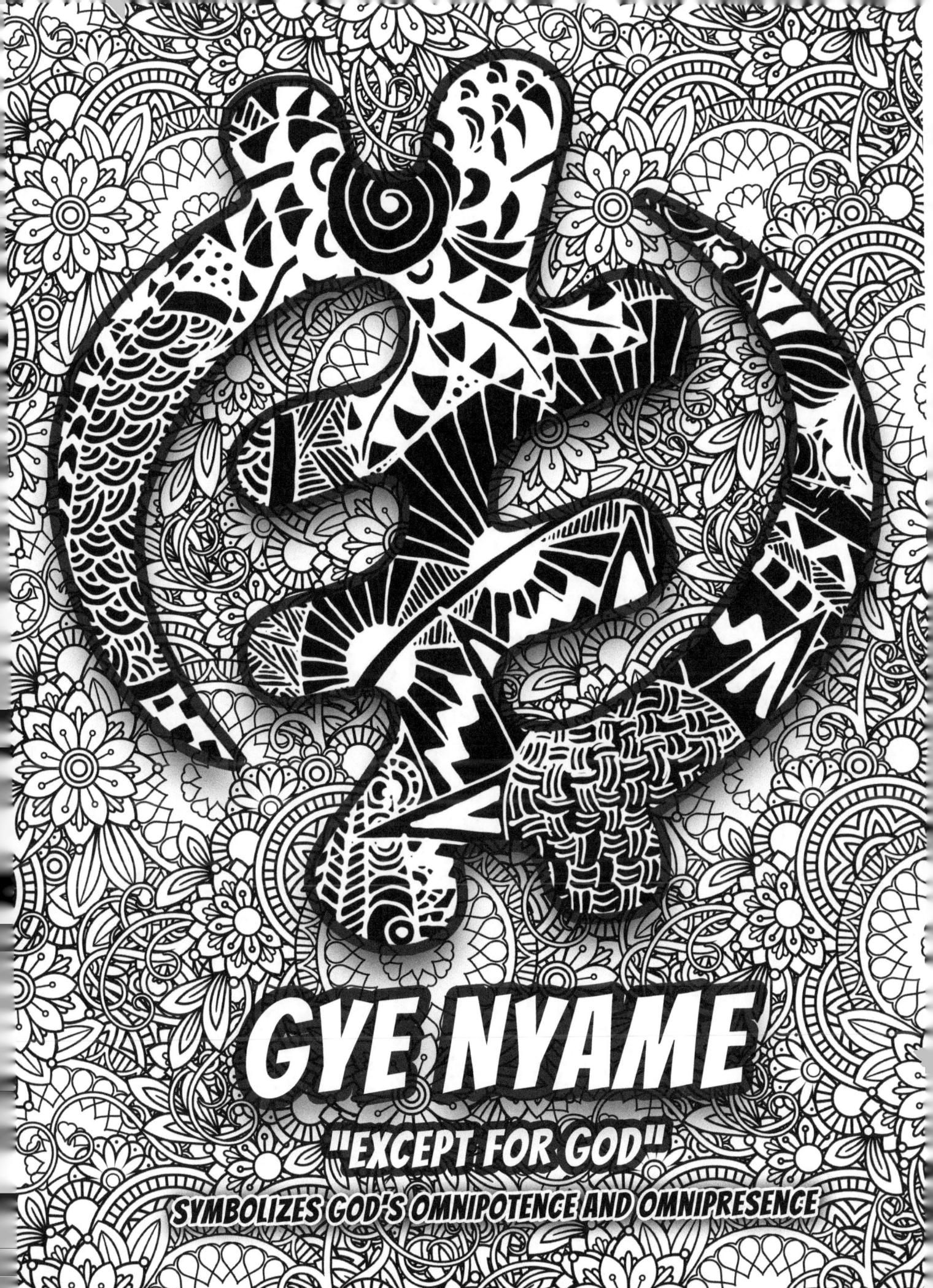

GYE NYAME

"EXCEPT FOR GOD"

SYMBOLIZES GOD'S OMNIPOTENCE AND OMNIPRESENCE

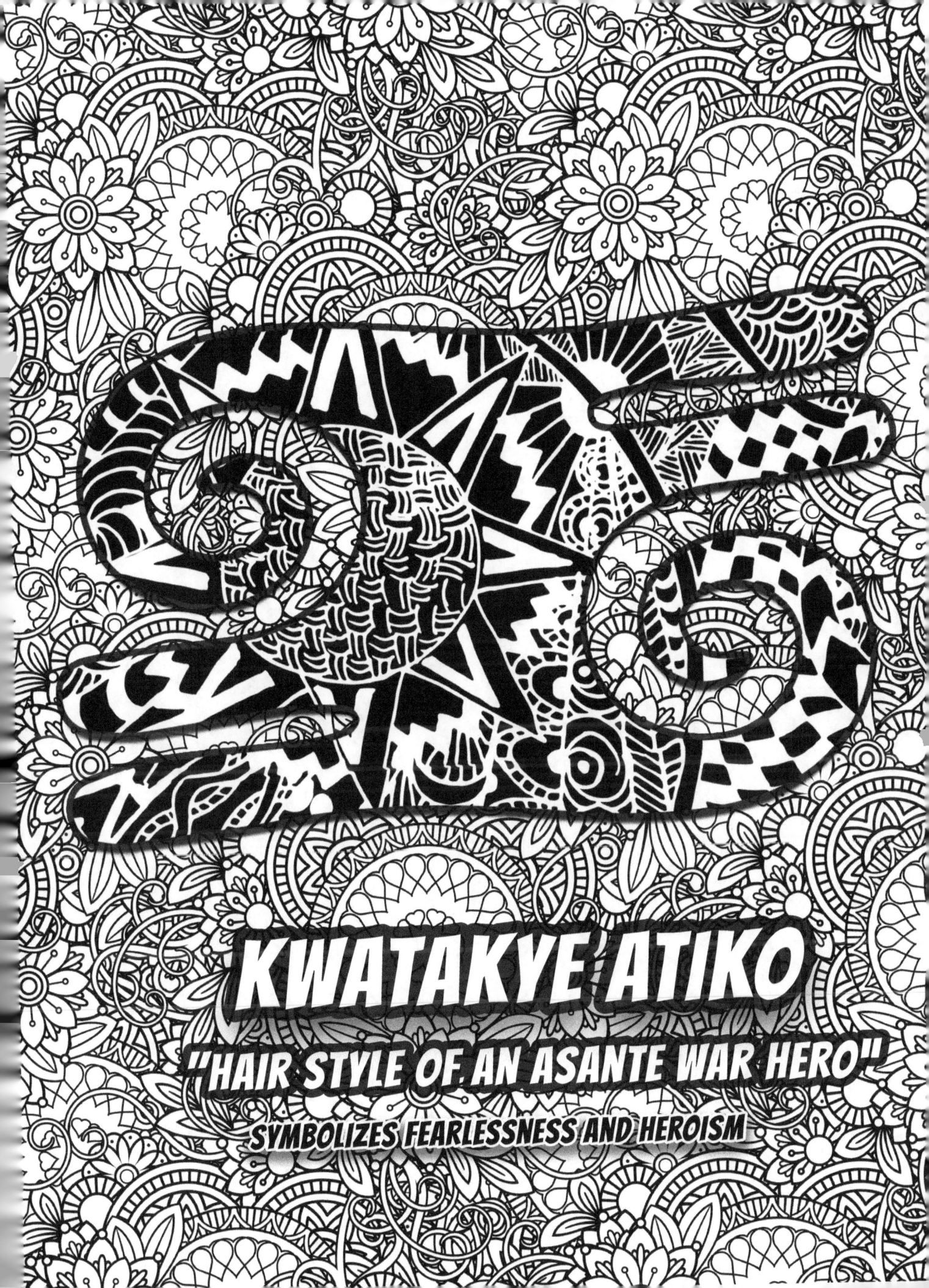

KWATAKYE ATIKO

"HAIR STYLE OF AN ASANTE WAR HERO"

SYMBOLIZES FEARLESSNESS AND HEROISM

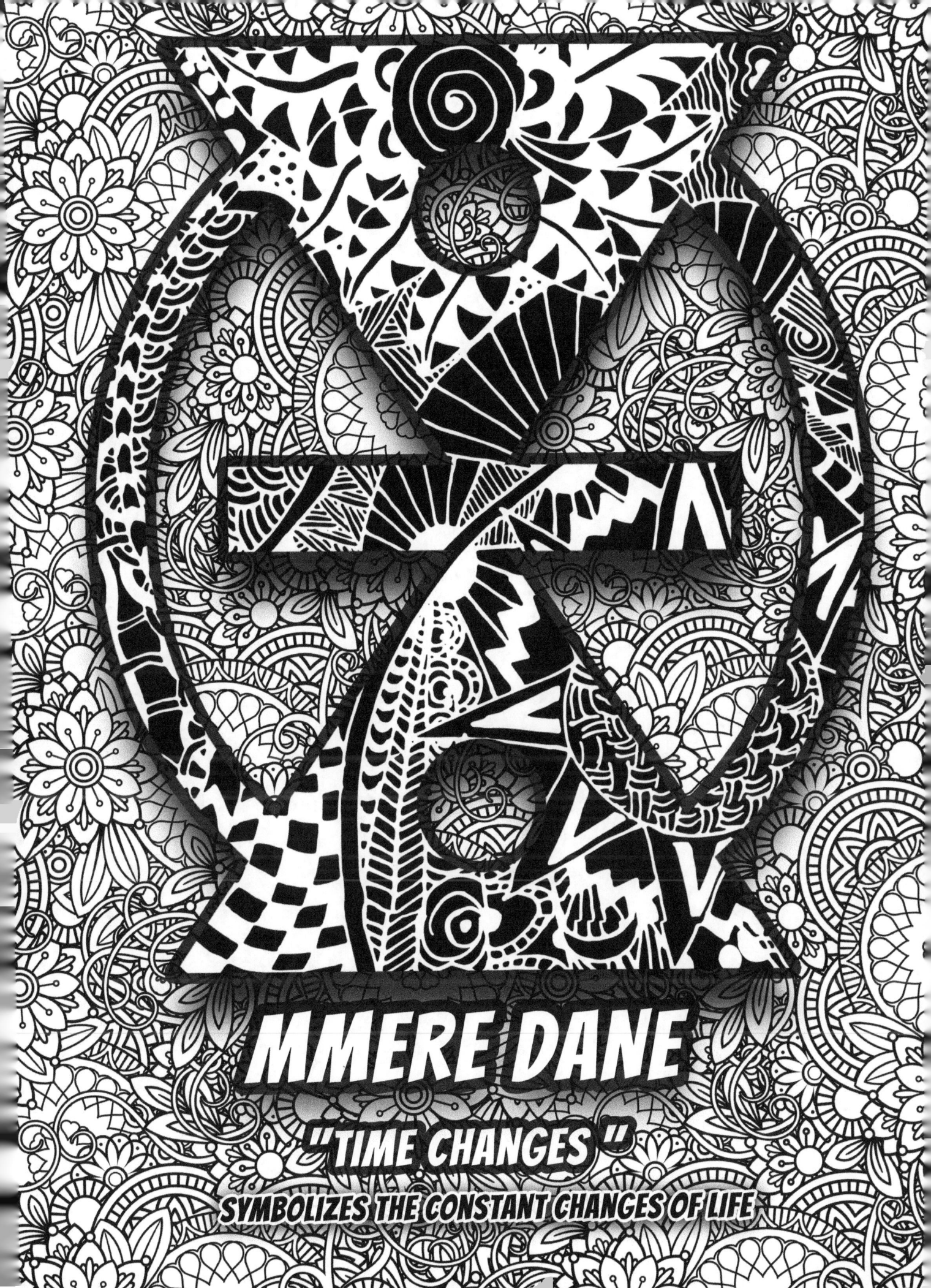

MMERE DANE

"TIME CHANGES"

SYMBOLIZES THE CONSTANT CHANGES OF LIFE

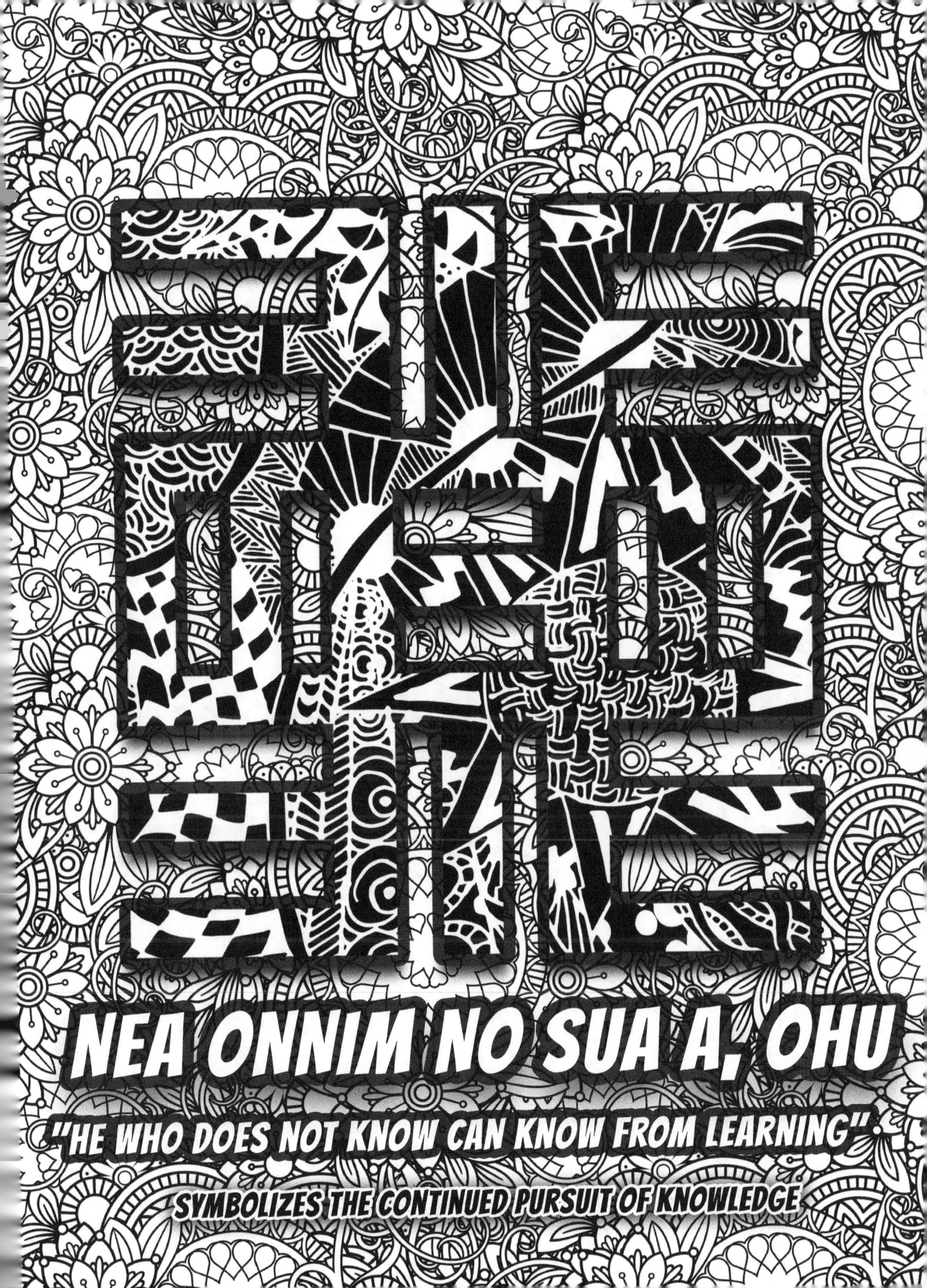

NEA ONNIM NO SUA A, OHU

"HE WHO DOES NOT KNOW CAN KNOW FROM LEARNING"

SYMBOLIZES THE CONTINUED PURSUIT OF KNOWLEDGE

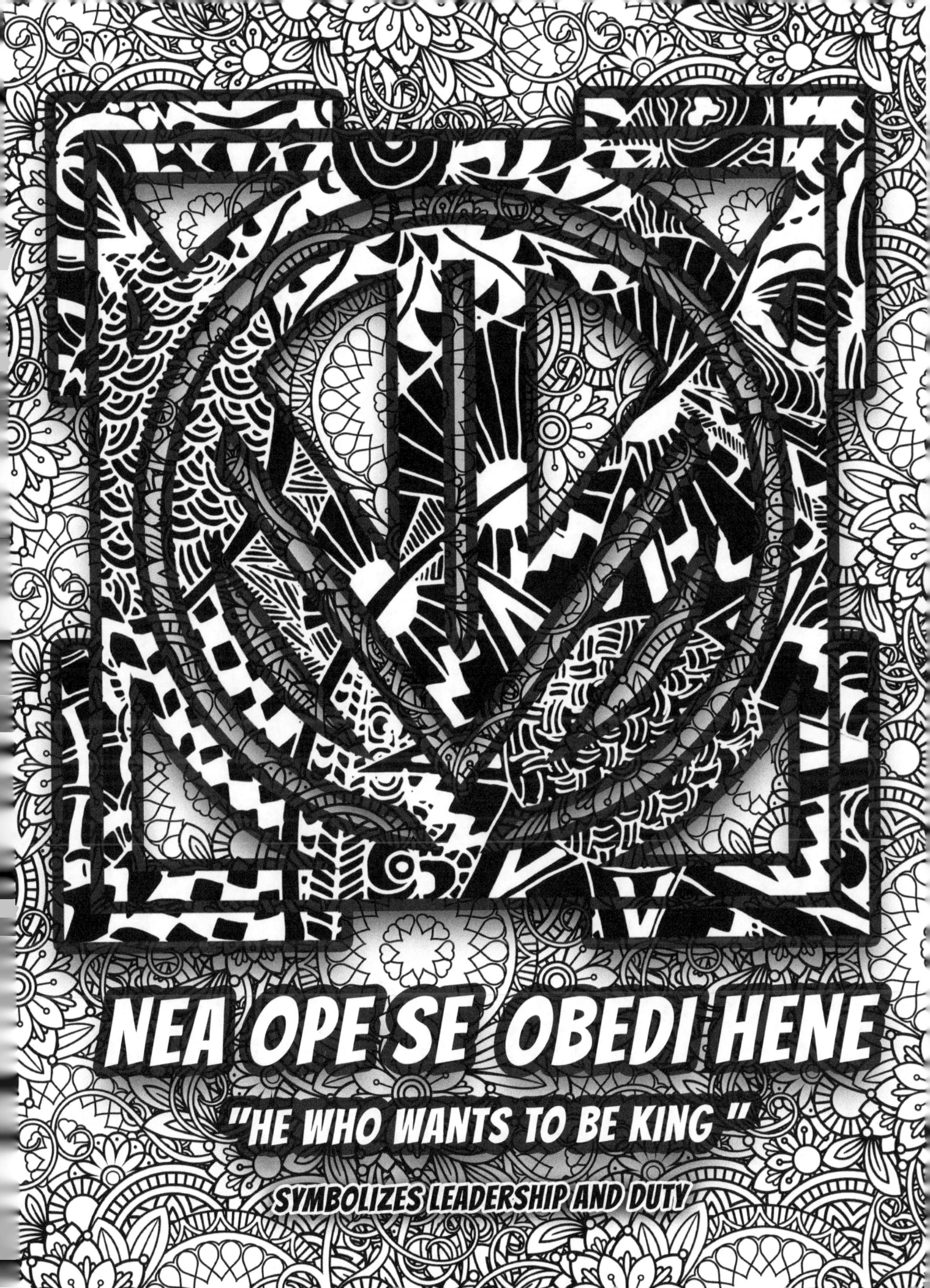

NEA OPE SE OBEDI HENE

"HE WHO WANTS TO BE KING"

SYMBOLIZES LEADERSHIP AND DUTY

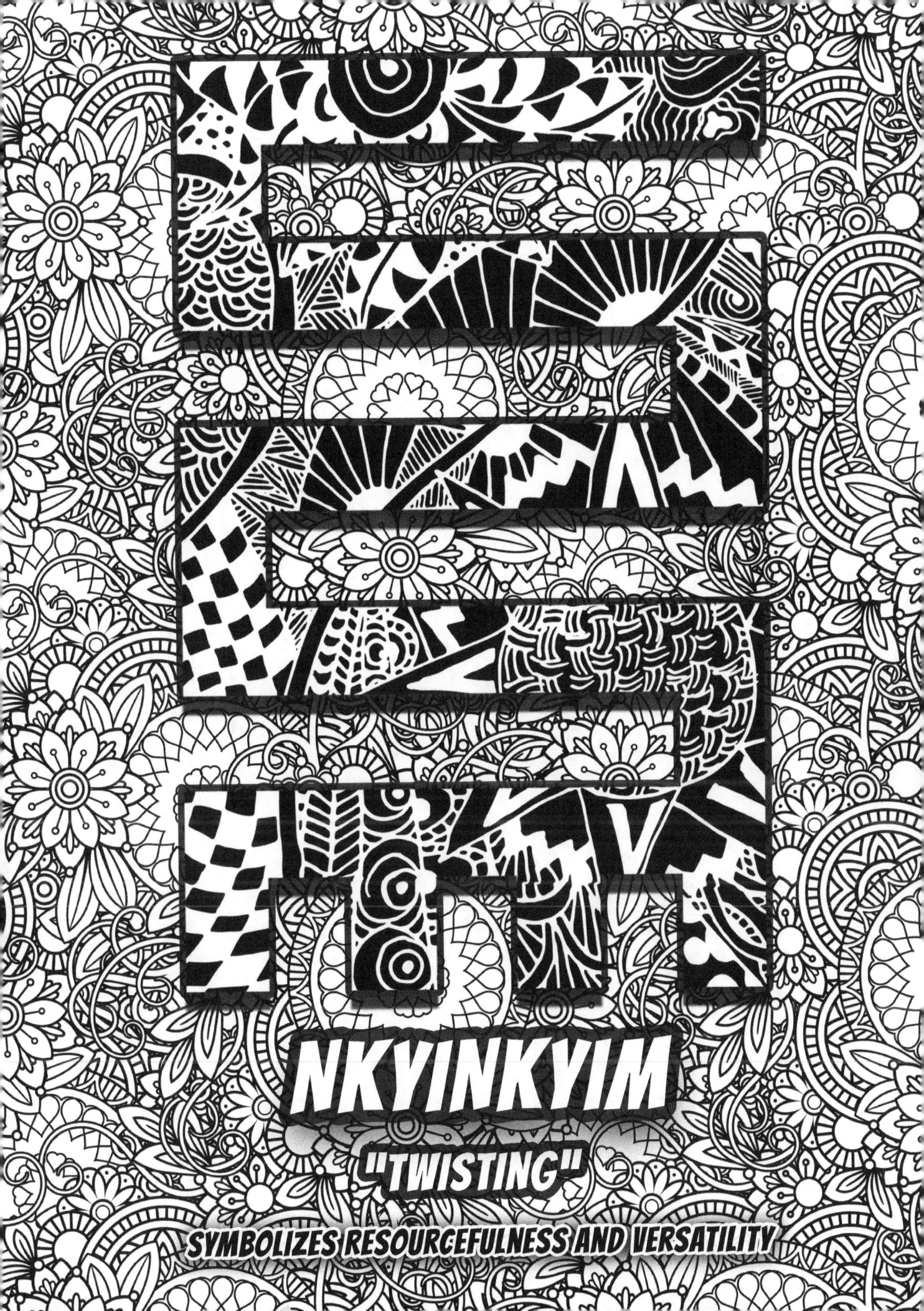

NKYINKYIM

"TWISTING"

SYMBOLIZES RESOURCEFULNESS AND VERSATILITY

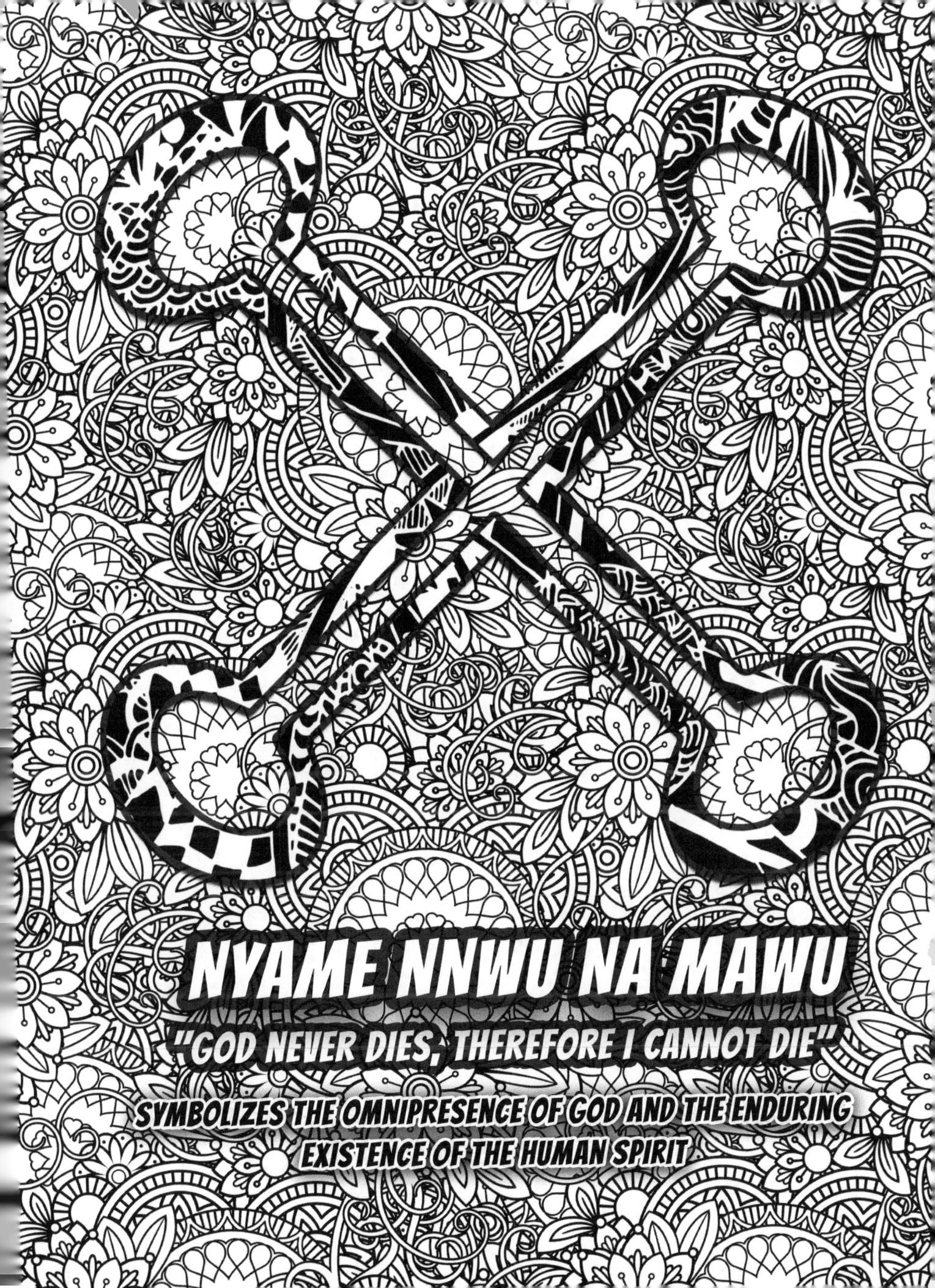

NYAME NNWU NA MAWU

"GOD NEVER DIES, THEREFORE I CANNOT DIE"

SYMBOLIZES THE OMNIPRESENCE OF GOD AND THE ENDURING
EXISTENCE OF THE HUMAN SPIRIT

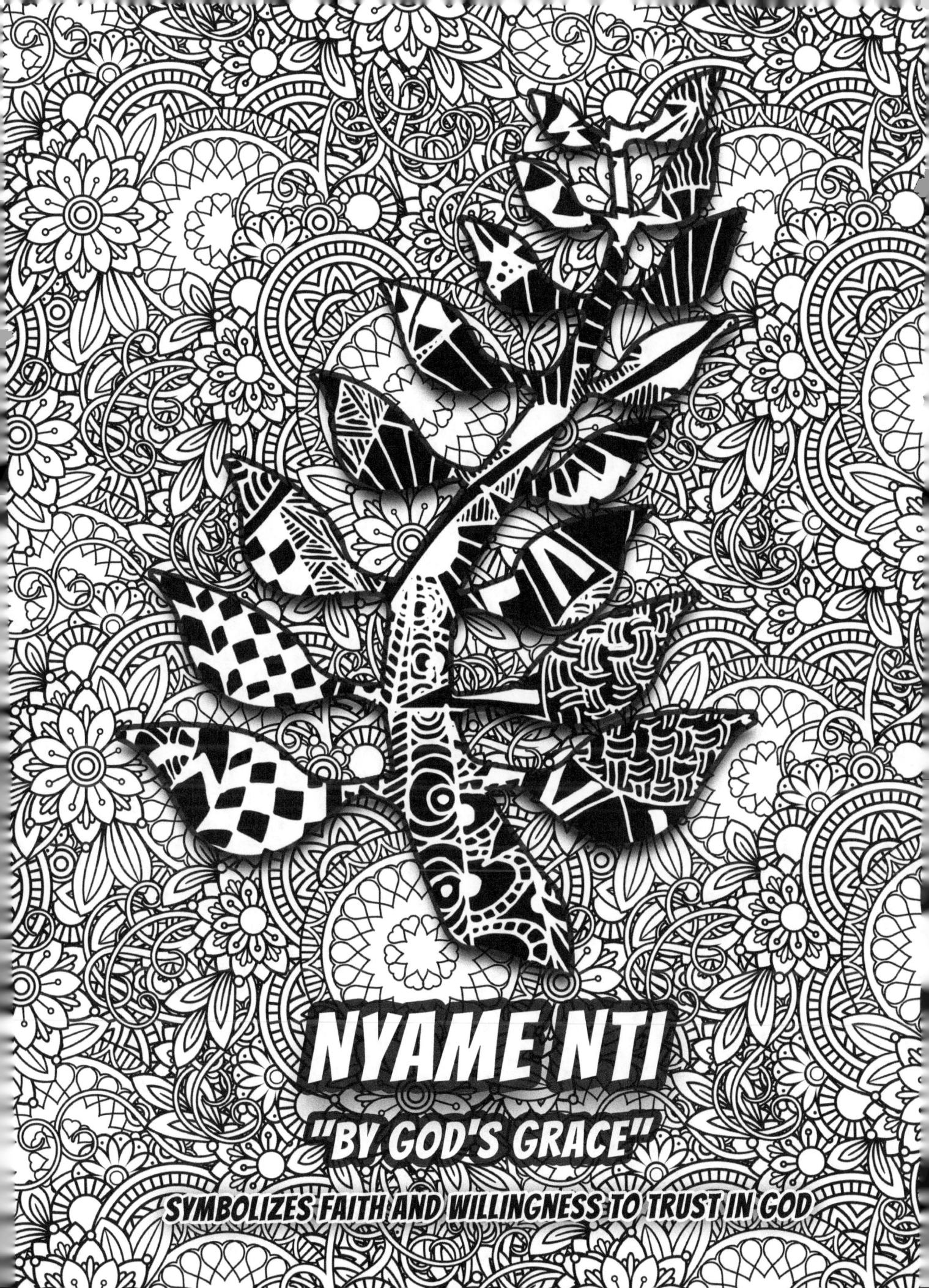

NYAME NTI

"BY GOD'S GRACE"

SYMBOLIZES FAITH AND WILLINGNESS TO TRUST IN GOD

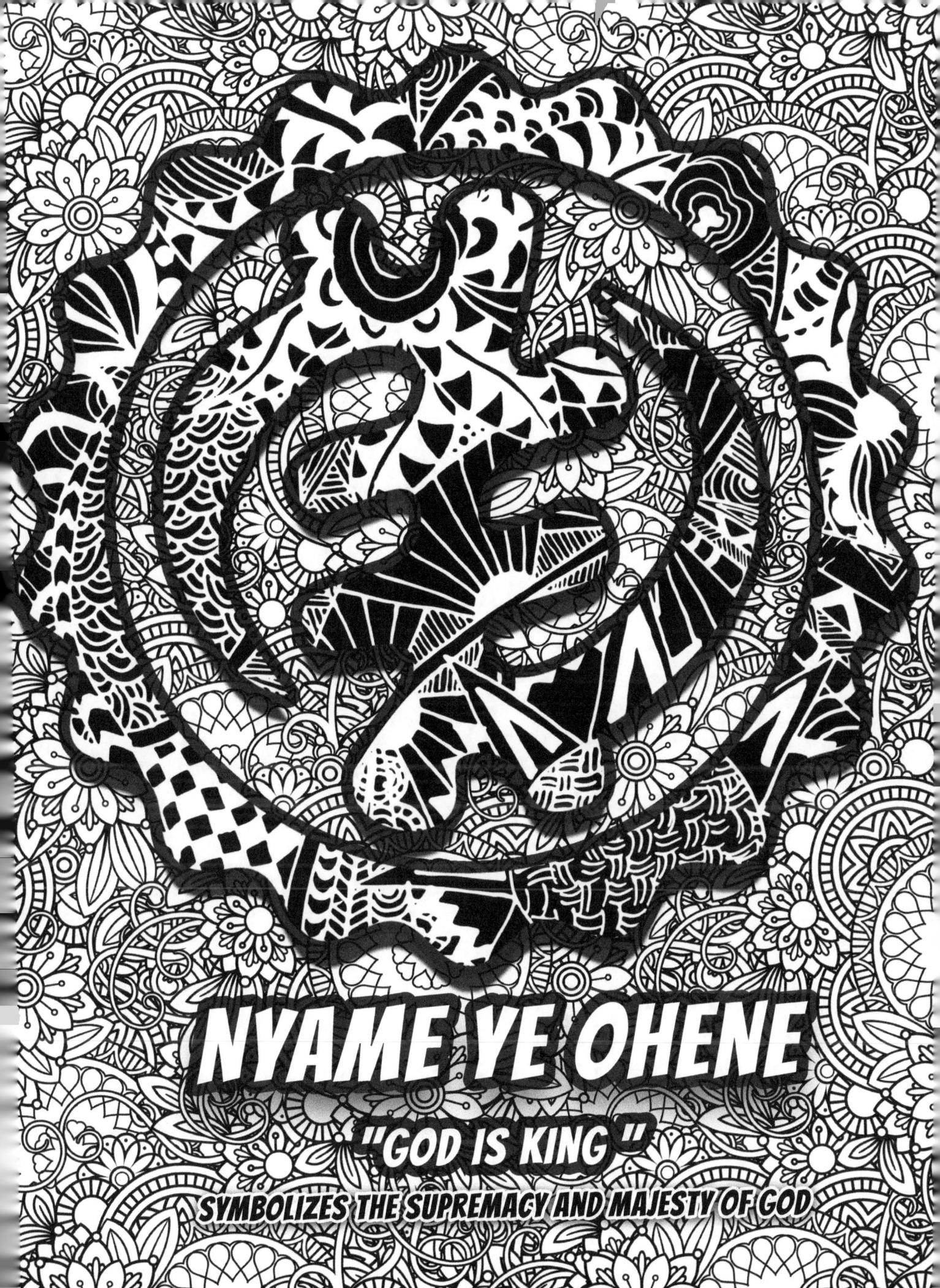

NYAME YE OHENE

"GOD IS KING"

SYMBOLIZES THE SUPREMACY AND MAJESTY OF GOD

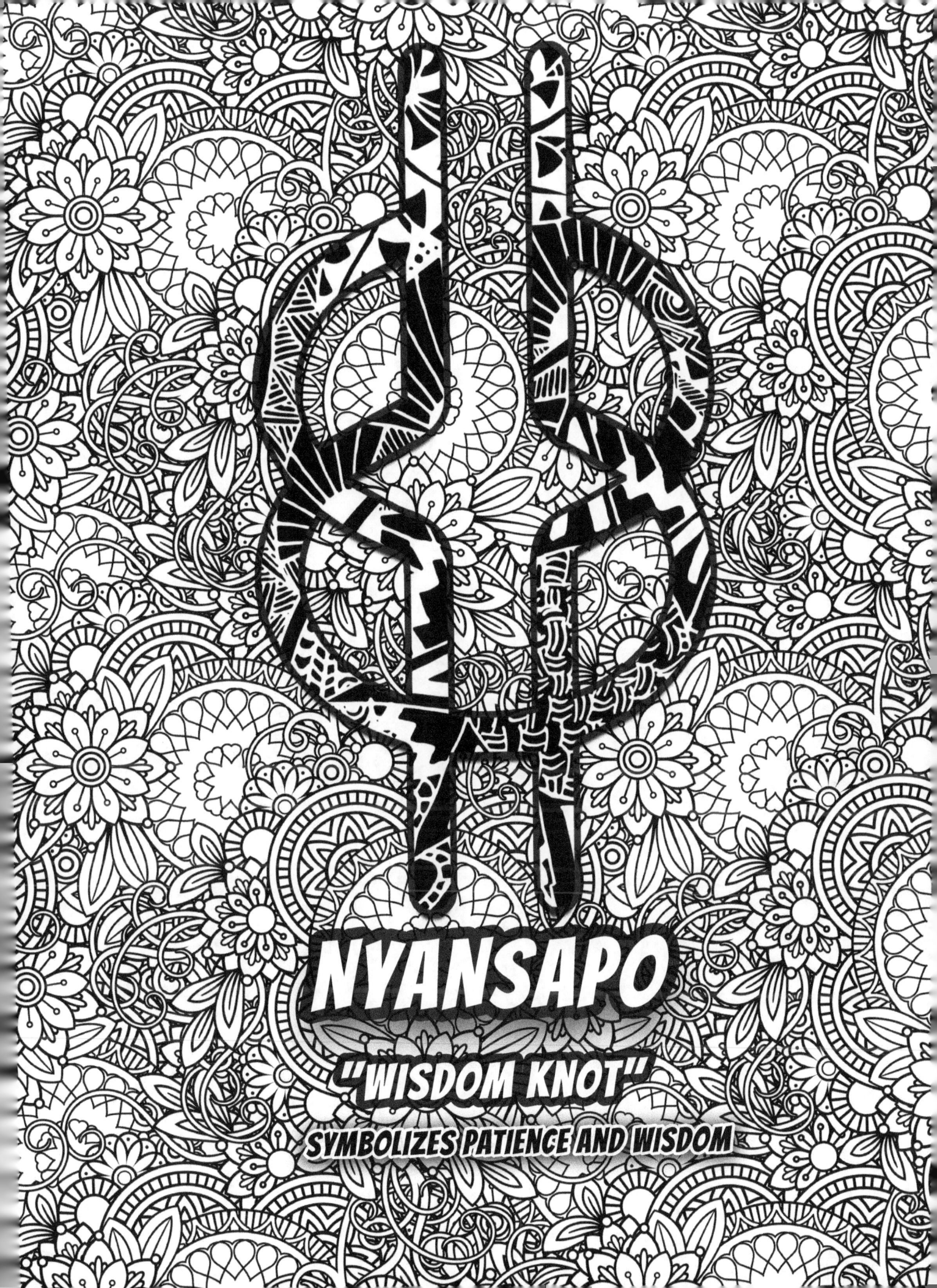

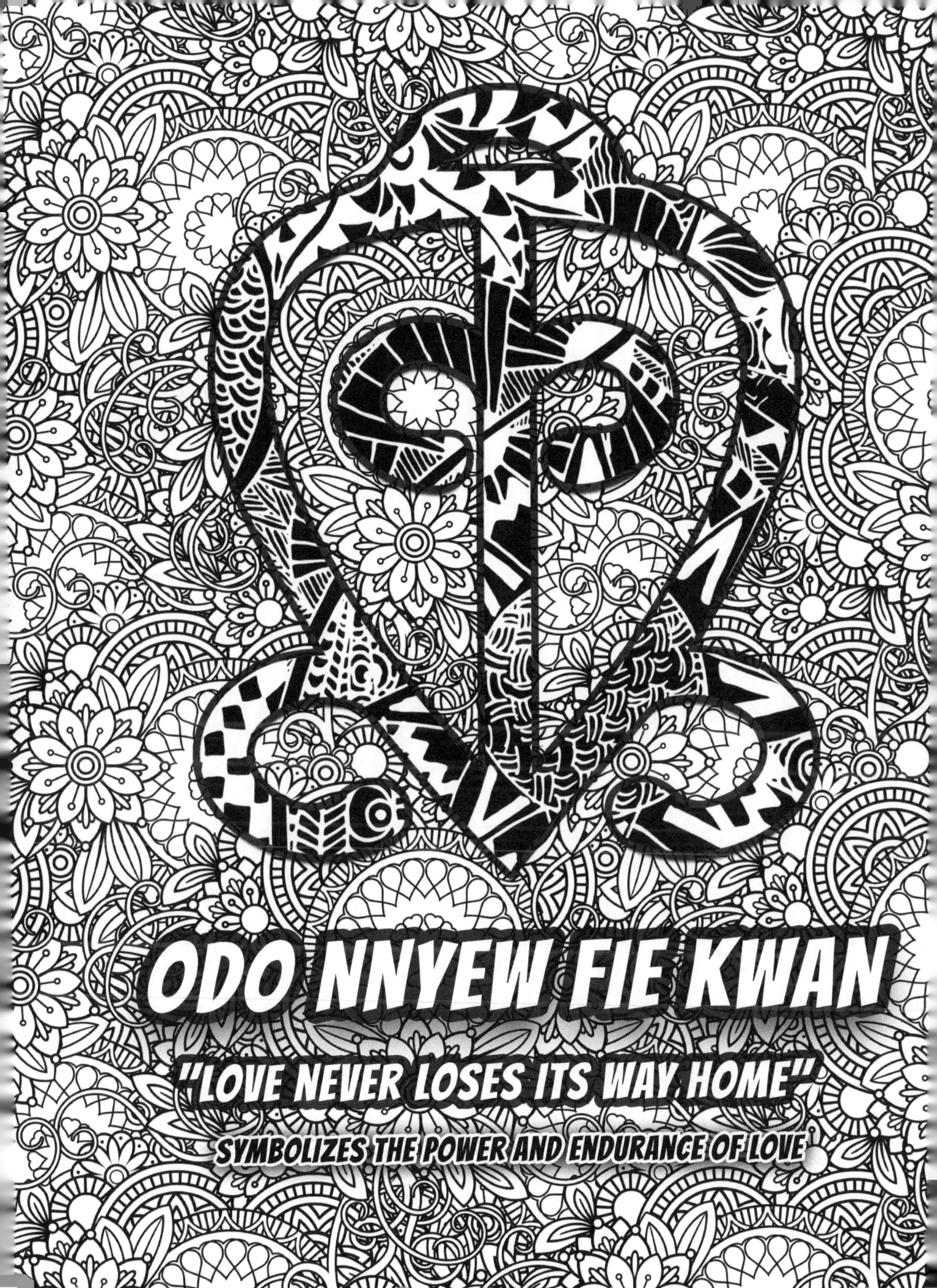

ODO NNYEW FIE KWAN

"LOVE NEVER LOSES ITS WAY, HOME"

SYMBOLIZES THE POWER AND ENDURANCE OF LOVE

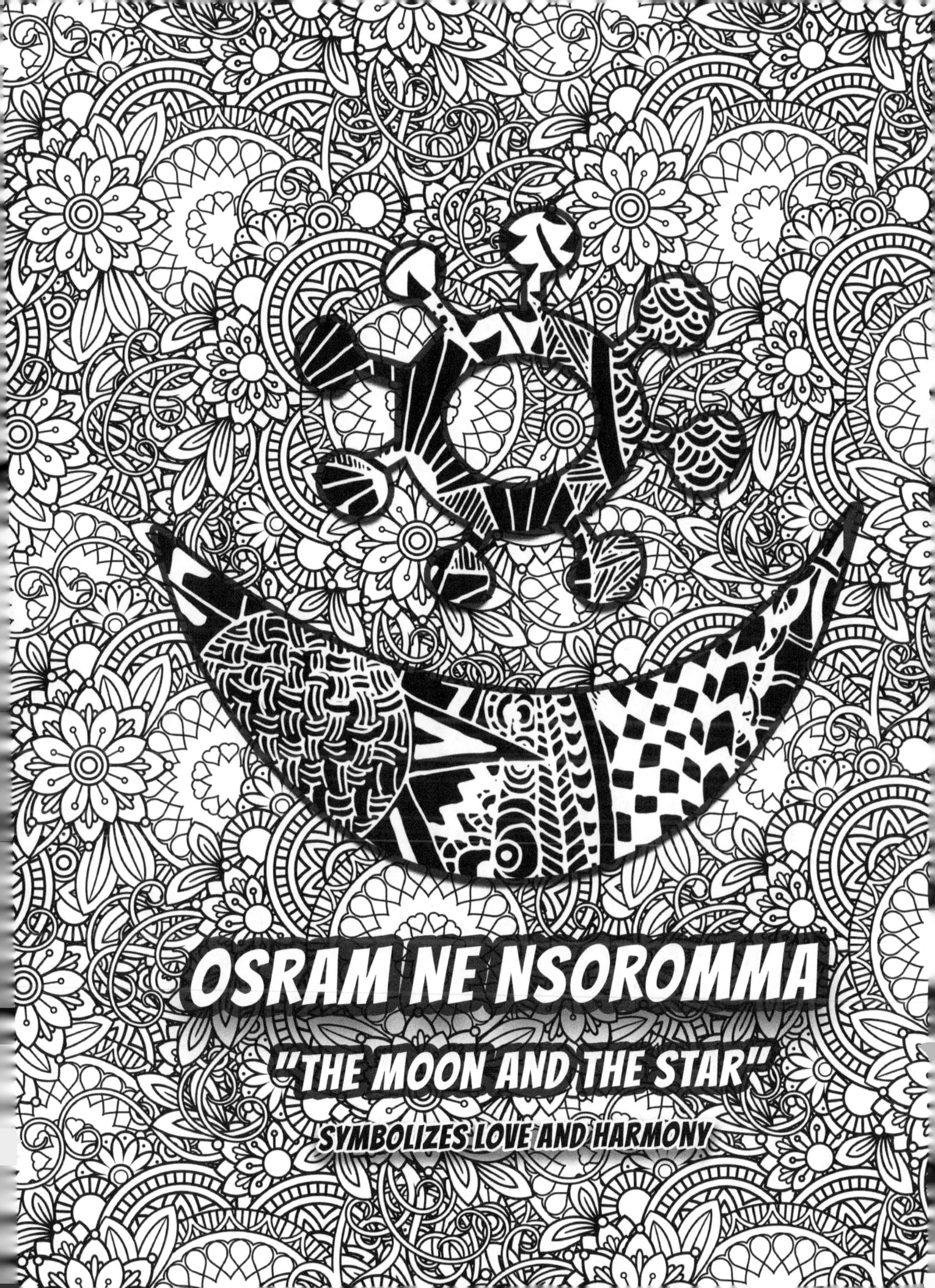

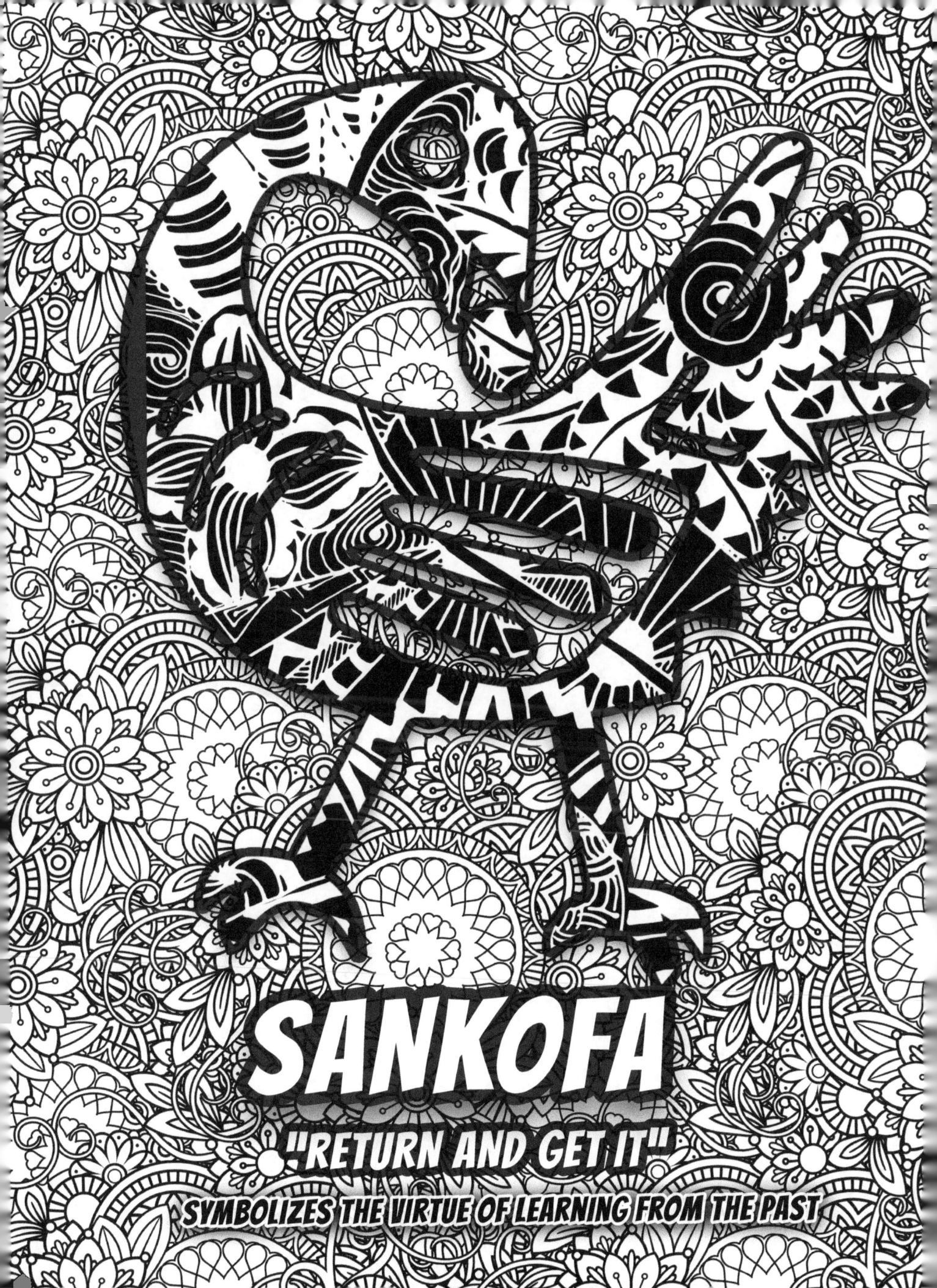

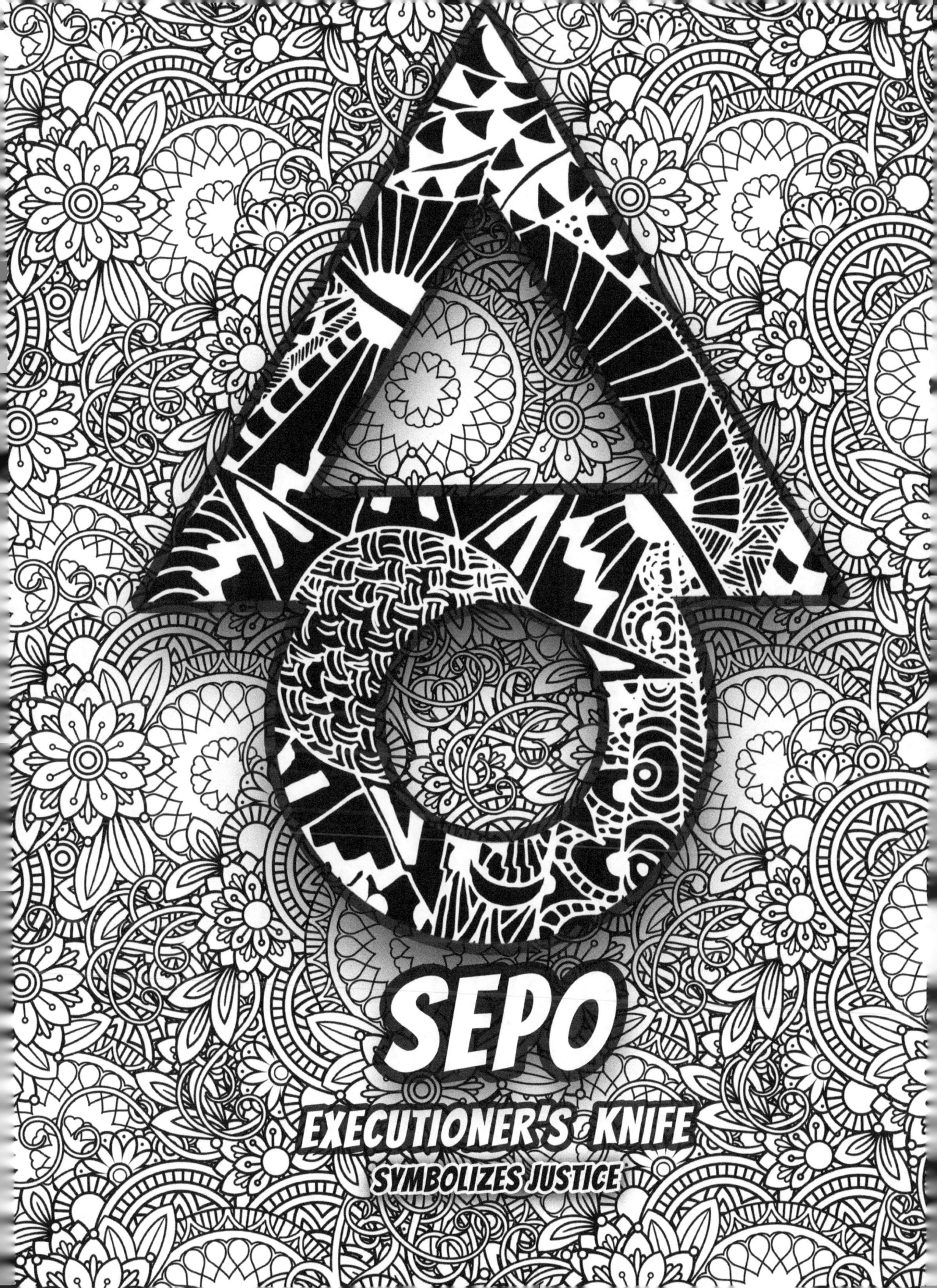

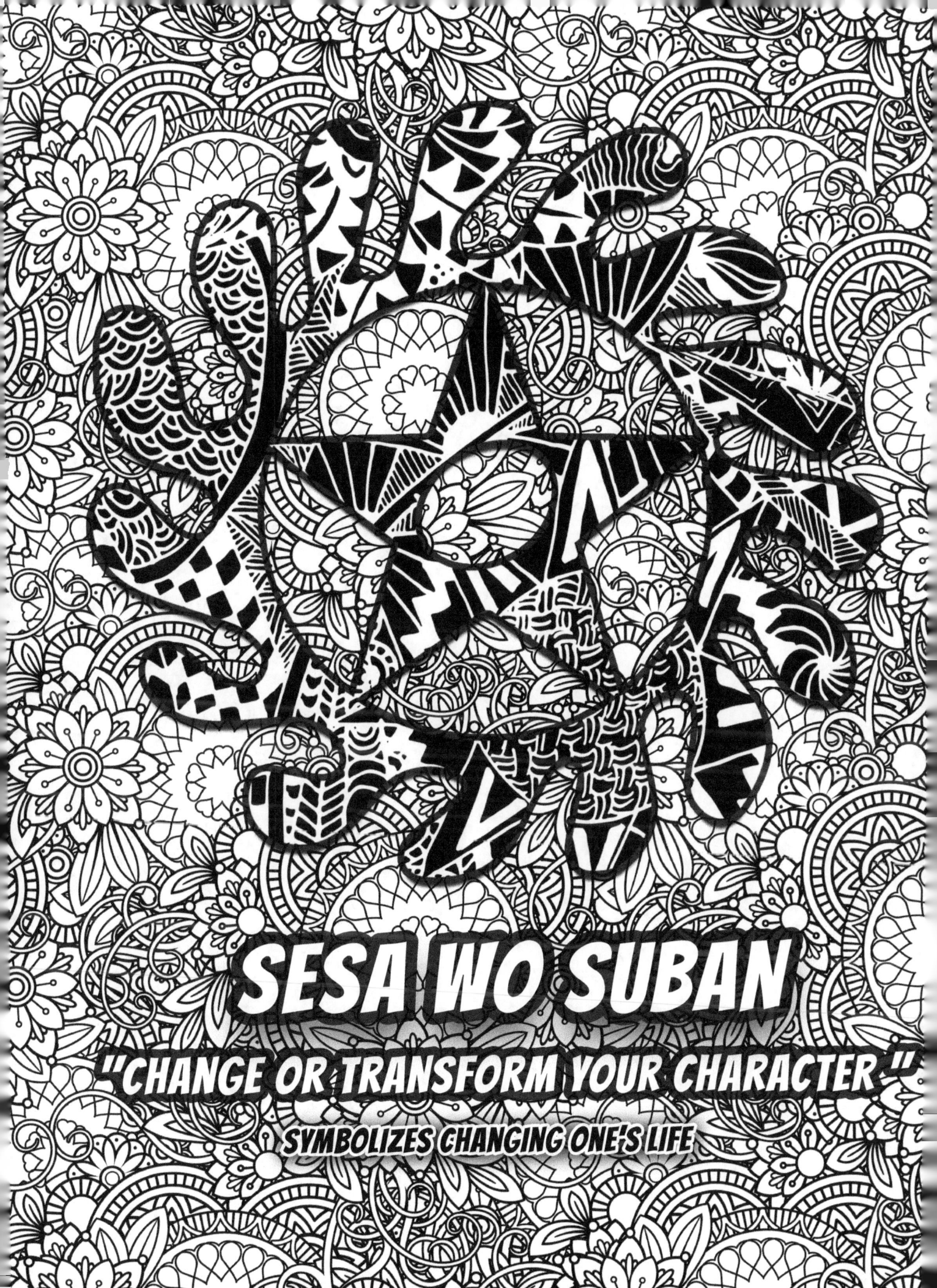

SESA WO SUBAN

"CHANGE OR TRANSFORM YOUR CHARACTER"

SYMBOLIZES CHANGING ONE'S LIFE

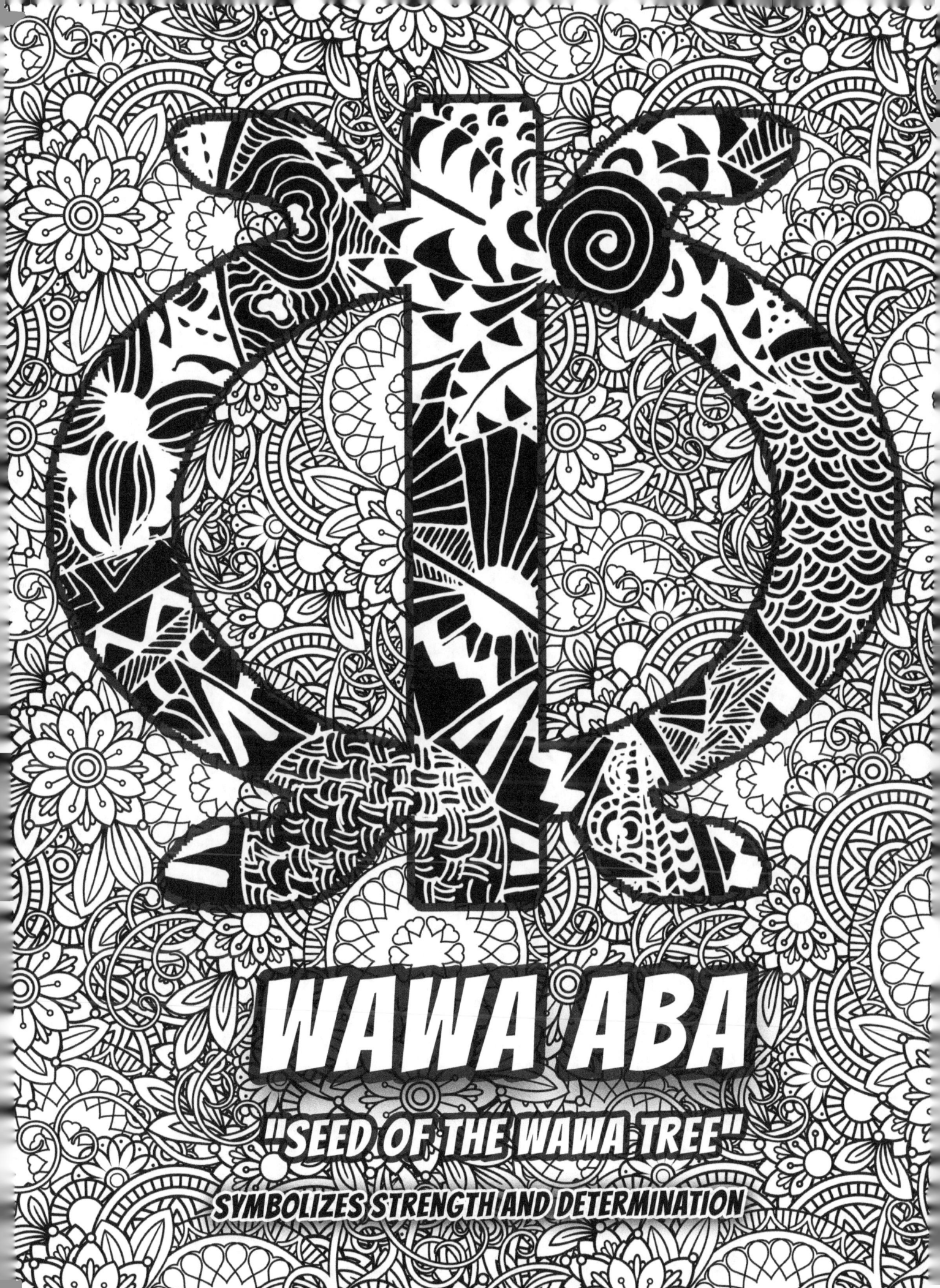

WAWA ABA

"SEED OF THE WAWA TREE"

SYMBOLIZES STRENGTH AND DETERMINATION

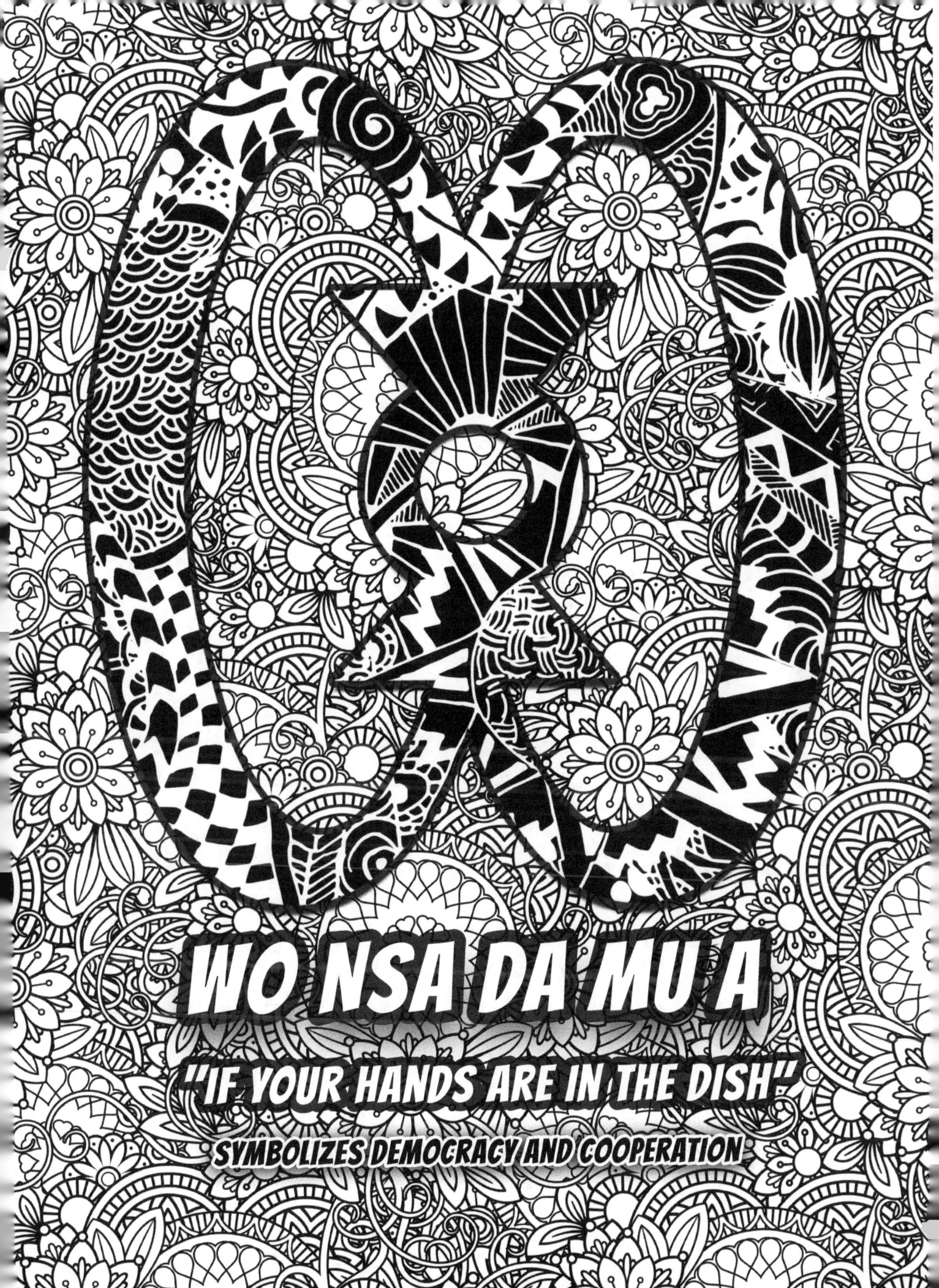

WO NSA DA MU A

"IF YOUR HANDS ARE IN THE DISH"

SYMBOLIZES DEMOCRACY AND COOPERATION